DATE DUE

THE AMERICAN CIVIL WAR AND RECONSTRUCTION

1850 to 1890

DOCUMENTING AMERICA
THE PRIMARY SOURCE DOCUMENTS OF A NATION

THE AMERICAN CIVIL WAR AND RECONSTRUCTION

1850 to 1890

EDITED BY JEFF WALLENFELDT, MANAGER, GEOGRAPHY AND HISTORY

Britannica®
Educational Publishing

IN ASSOCIATION WITH

ROSEN
EDUCATIONAL SERVICES

Published in 2012 by Britannica Educational Publishing
(a trademark of Encyclopædia Britannica, Inc.)
in association with Rosen Educational Services, LLC
29 East 21st Street, New York, NY 10010.

Distributed exclusively by Rosen Educational Services.
For a listing of additional Britannica Educational Publishing titles, call toll free (800) 237-9932.

First Edition

Britannica Educational Publishing
Michael I. Levy: Executive Editor
Adam Augustyn: Assistant Manager, Encyclopædia Britannica
Marilyn L. Barton: Senior Coordinator, Production Control
Steven Bosco: Director, Editorial Technologies
Lisa S. Braucher: Senior Producer and Data Editor
Yvette Charboneau: Senior Copy Editor
Kathy Nakamura: Manager, Media Acquisition
Jeff Wallenfeldt: Manager, Geography and History

Rosen Educational Services
Hope Lourie Killcoyne: Executive Editor
Nelson Sá: Art Director
Cindy Reiman: Photography Manager
Matthew Cauli: Cover Design
Brian Garvey: Designer
Introduction by Jeff Wallenfeldt

Library of Congress Cataloging-in-Publication Data

The American Civil War and Reconstruction: 1850 to 1890/edited by Jeff Wallenfeldt.
—1st ed.
    p. cm.—(Documenting America: the primary source documents of a nation)
"In association with Britannica Educational Publishing, Rosen Educational Services."
Includes bibliographical references and index.
ISBN 978-1-61530-680-0 (library binding)
1. United States—History—Civil War, 1861-1865—Sources. 2. Reconstruction (U.S. history,
1865-1877)—Sources. 3. United States—History—1849-1877—Sources. I. Wallenfeldt, Jeffrey H.
E464.A415 2012
973.7—dc23

2011026695

Manufactured in the United States of America

On the cover: The Battle of Gettysburg in July 1863 was a major defeat for Confederate
Gen. Robert E. Lee; thereafter the war turned in favour of the Union. *MPI/Archive Photos/
Getty Images*. Emancipation Proclamation. *General Records of the U.S. Government, Natural
Archives, Washington, D.C.*

On pages viii-ix: Oil on canvas portrait of Abraham Lincoln by George Healy, 1887.
Katherine Young/Hulton Archive/Getty Images

On pages 1, 19, 33, 49, 66: President Lincoln and his Cabinet at the signing of the
Emancipation Proclamation, which declared that slaves in Southern states would be "thenceforward, and forever, free." *MPI/Archive Photos/Getty Images*

CONTENTS

45

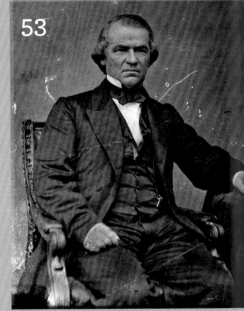

53

59

62

"A house divided cannot stand."
"The better angels of our nature."
"A government of the people, by the people and for the people shall not perish from the earth."

These statements are the much-noted and long-remembered words of Abraham Lincoln, the 16th president of the United States, the unconventionally majestic figure who towers still over the era of the American Civil War. Unschooled, though anything but unlettered, the shrewdest of country bumpkins, Lincoln conveyed his boundless compassion and moral authority in a rhetorical eloquence fashioned from the works of William Shakespeare, the Bible, and hundreds of spellbinding tales told on the Illinois court circuit by an ungainly, often melancholy lawyer who came to life and lifted spirits as a storyteller.

There is no better place to begin than Lincoln's words to try to come to grips with this period of American history that continues to send aftershocks into the 21st century. This volume provides several opportunities to listen closely to Lincoln. Yet as elegant and influential as Lincoln's speeches and writing were, his was but one voice in the conflict that tore the United States in two. Equally telling are the words of Lincoln's allies and adversaries, as well as those of Americans, famous and not so famous, who preceded and followed his relatively short appearance on the stage of 19th century history, playing their own important roles in the American saga. Then, as now, those with the ability to move people with their oration possessed great power. This volume uses some of the era's most memorable speeches to take the reader deep into the issues and events surrounding the Civil War and Reconstruction, but it also employs a selection of legislation, legal documents, letters, poetry, fiction, and lyrics to further illustrate the moment. A narrative, offering description and analysis, guides the reader through the period and provides a framework for exploring the primary source documents. When these documents are short, they are presented whole within the narrative; more often, excerpts are provided that give a flavour of the document, which is presented more fully in the Appendix.

What is to be done about slavery? That question, asked since the founding of the United States, had heated up several times on the way to reaching the boiling point in the 1850s. In the early days of the republic, slaves toiled throughout the country, but by mid-century slavery had been abolished in the North, while in the South the "peculiar institution," as it was euphemistically referred to, had become ever more important to the region's economy and way of life. The Missouri Compromise of 1820 and the Compromise of 1850 had placated the contending factions, maintaining the balance of political power between the slave and non-slave states and carefully delineating where slavery could be practiced and where it could not in the new territories acquired by the country.

But in the 1850s, as the abolition movement began to gain steam—fuelled by Harriet Beecher Stowe's evocative depiction of the cruelty of slavery in her novel *Uncle Tom's Cabin* (1853)—the matter of the extension of slavery in the West was again centre stage. Stephen Douglas, a Democratic senator from Illinois, shepherded through Congress the Kansas-Nebraska Act (1854), making popular sovereignty the law of the land, by which the residents of the new territories would decide themselves whether to permit slavery. In "Bleeding Kansas" the contest between advocates and opponents of slavery erupted into open warfare. Responding to what he saw as the consummation of "The Crime Against Kansas," Sen. Charles Sumner of Massachusetts, an ardent abolitionist, said, "Slavery now stands erect, clanking its chains on the territory of Kansas, surrounded by a code of death, and trampling upon all cherished liberties, whether of speech, the press, the bar, the trial by jury, or the electoral franchise." So outraged by the speech from which these remarks were taken was Rep. Preston S. Brooks of South Carolina that he attacked Sumner with a cane on the Senate floor.

The abolitionist cause received another blow when the U.S. Supreme Court in 1857 ruled against Dred Scott, a slave who had sued for his freedom because he had been taken to live for a time in a non-slave state. In the majority opinion, Chief Justice Roger B. Taney wrote that black people "had for more than a century before been regarded as beings of an inferior order and altogether unfit to associate with the white race, either in social or political relations; and so far inferior that they had no rights which the white man was bound to respect."

Among those who took issue with the ruling in the *Dred Scott* case was Lincoln, who launched his senatorial campaign against Douglas in June 1858 at the Illinois state convention of the new anti-slavery Republican Party with his "House Divided" speech, in which he declared, "I believe this government cannot endure permanently, half slave and half free. I do not expect the Union to be dissolved; I do not expect the house to fall; but I do expect it will cease to be divided. It will become all one thing, or all the other." The famous Lincoln-Douglas debates that followed resulted in Douglass's reelection but brought Lincoln national attention.

In 1859 John Brown—who was responsible for the Pottawatomie Massacre of 1856 in Bleeding Kansas—led an unsuccessful raid on the federal arsenal in Harpers Ferry, Va. (now W. Va.). He had hoped to launch a massive slave rebellion, but though he failed, he enraged and terrified Southern slave owners. Hanged for his actions, Brown also became an abolitionist martyr, likened to English Puritan hero Oliver Cromwell by Transcendentalist Henry David Thoreau, who said of Brown, "No man has appeared in America, as yet, who loved his fellow-man so well and treated him so tenderly. He lived for him. He took up his life and he laid it down for him."

When Lincoln, the surprising nominee of the Republican Party, was elected president in 1860, the die was cast. Even before he took office, the secession had begun of the 11 states that would constitute the Confederacy, whose unofficial poet laureate, Henry Timrod, exalted the heritage and valour of its land and people in "Ethnogenesis." In his inaugural address, Lincoln made clear that he would not allow the Union to be sundered, but he also reached across the Mason-Dixon Line, saying, "We are not enemies but friends. Though passion may have strained, it must not break our bonds of affection. The mystic chords of memory, stretching from every battlefield and patriot grave to every living heart and hearthstone all over this broad land, will yet swell the chorus of the Union, when again touched, as surely they will be, by the better angels of our nature."

But mortal enemies the North and South had become, marching off to the strains of "The Bonnie Blue Flag" ("For Southern rights, hurrah!") and "The Battle-Cry of Freedom" ("The Union forever, hurrah! boys, hurrah!") to fight in a protracted four-year civil war. More than 600,000 would die in what was seen by many as the first truly modern war, in which death, as later explained by onetime Union soldier Frank Wilkeson, sometimes came quickly and horribly and other times slowly and quietly: "Dying soldiers seldom called on those who were dearest to them, seldom conjured their Northern or Southern homes, until they became delirious. Then, when their minds wandered and fluttered at the approach of freedom, they babbled of their homes. Some were boys again and were fishing in Northern trout streams...Some were with their wives and children..." Walt Whitman's poem "Come Up from the Fields Father" functions as a sort of mournful home-front response to Wilkeson's description: "Alas poor boy, he will never be better (nor maybe needs to better, that brave and simple soul),/ While they stand at home at the door he is dead already."

From the war's outset, abolitionists demanded it be fought not only to restore the Union but also to bring about immediate emancipation. John S. Rock, an African American physician and attorney, debunked both the notion that slaves would not know how to handle freedom as well as the logic of fighting solely for reconciliation. "The government wishes to bring back the country to what it was before...but what is to be gained by it?" he asked in a speech in 1862. "If we are fools enough to retain the cancer that is eating out our vitals, when we can safely extirpate it, who will pity us if we see our mistake when we are past recovery?" On the other side, the Peace Democrats, or Copperheads, led by Rep. Clement Vallandigham of Ohio, bemoaned the financial and human cost of the war and called for its end. In the middle of all this was Lincoln, orchestrating much of the war's strategy himself, trying to find a Union general who could lead dynamically, and finally declaring the Emancipation Proclamation in 1863 as much for military reasons (depriving the South of its greatest resource, paving the way for the important contribution of African American troops to the Union war effort) as for humanitarian ones.

In 1863 Union forces won huge victories at Vicksburg, Miss., and Gettysburg, Pa., which hastened the end of the war. At the commemoration of the Gettysburg battlefield cemetery, Lincoln called on the living "to be here dedicated to the great task remaining before us—that from these honored dead we take increased devotion to that cause for which they gave the last full measure of devotion; that we here highly resolve that these dead shall not have died in vain; that this nation, under God, shall have a new birth of freedom…" In his second inaugural address, before reaching out "with malice toward none, with charity for all…to bind up the nation's wounds," Lincoln confirmed the purpose of the war rapidly drawing to a close, saying, "Yet, if God wills that it [the war] continue until all the wealth piled upon the bondsman's 250 years of unrequited toil shall be sunk, and until every drop of blood drawn with the lash shall be paid by another drawn with the sword, as was said 3,000 years ago, so still it must be said, 'The judgments of the Lord are true and righteous together.'" A little more than a month later, on the eve of Gen. Robert E. Lee's surrender to Gen. Ulysses S. Grant, Gen. George Pickett, who led the final valiant Confederate charge at Gettysburg, wrote to his wife, "It is finished! Ah, my beloved division! Thousands of them have gone to their eternal home, having given up their lives for the cause they knew to be just…We have poured out our blood, and suffered untold hardships and privations, all in vain."

The war was effectively over, but before the last troops had surrendered, Confederate sympathizer and actor John Wilkes Booth assassinated Lincoln, changing the way that peace would be waged. Lincoln's plan for reincorporating the South into the Union was straightforward, requiring that a state emancipate its slaves and that at least one-tenth of its voters embrace the Constitution. Radicals within his party, determined that measures be put in place to guarantee the rights of the emancipated slaves, clashed with Lincoln's successor, Vice Pres. Andrew Johnson, a Tennessean who took a more conciliatory approach toward the former states of the Confederacy. When Johnson vetoed the bill creating the Freedman's Bureau to aid the freed slaves, Congress overrode that veto. Responding to criticism of his veto, Johnson asked, "While conscious, intelligent traitors are to be punished, should whole states, communities, and people be made to submit to and bear the penalty of death?…I say that when these states comply with the Constitution, when they have given sufficient evidence of their loyalty and that they can be trusted, when they yield obedience to the law, I say, extend to them the right band of fellowship, and let peace and union be restored." Congress's Joint Committee on Reconstruction, dominated by Rep. Thaddeus Stevens of Pennsylvania, was much less forgiving: "In return for our kind desire for the resumption of fraternal relations we receive only an insolent assumption of rights and privileges long since forfeited. The crime we have punished is paraded as virtue, and the principles of republican government which we have vindicated at so terrible a cost are denounced as unjust and oppressive."

It was the Radical Republicans' vision that triumphed in legislation such as the Civil Rights Act of 1866. The most prominent statutes of the act would later become part of the Constitution as the Fourteenth Amendment, but pivotal to the imposition of Radical Reconstruction in the South was the clause permitting its enforcement: "That it shall be lawful for the President of the United States, or such person as he may empower for that purpose, to employ such part of the land or naval forces of the United States, or of the militia, as shall be necessary to prevent the violation and enforce the due execution of this act." Military districts were created in the South, and the military endeavoured to protect both the civil rights of African Americans and their right to vote, guaranteed by the enactment of the Fifteenth Amendment. In the process, there was a brief but extraordinary flowering of democracy in the South, which saw African Americans assume a wide range of elected local and state offices and win seats in the U.S. House of Representatives and the Senate. When clandestine white supremacist groups such as the Knights of the White Camelia and the Ku Klux Klan struck back with terrorist tactics, the administration of

Pres. Ulysses S. Grant retaliated, its enforcement actions justified by a federal grand jury report noting that "many of the men who were openly and publicly speaking against the Klan, and pretending to deplore the work of this murderous conspiracy, were influential members of the order and directing its operations, even in detail."

By the late 1870s Northern zeal for Southern change had waned. Reconstruction came to an end with the withdrawal of federal troops and the gradual re-imposition of white rule. Soon Jim Crow laws and "separate but equal" hypocrisy that denied African Americans the vote and segregated Southern society were the order of the day. In 1883 Frederick Douglas, a prominent abolitionist and the country's most influential black spokesperson, described the "color line" that met an African American "everywhere, and in a measure shuts him out for all respectable and profitable trades and callings." As the century drew near a close, in 1895, in a speech that became known as the Atlanta Compromise, educator Booker T. Washington encouraged African Americans to apply themselves as artisans and labourers, and whites to support them in these efforts, calming white fears by saying, "In all things that are purely social we can be as separate as the fingers, yet one as the hand in all things essential to mutual progress." Other African American leaders such as W.E.B. Dubois saw Washington's approach as overly accommodationist, but DuBois's greatest moments were yet to come in the new American century.

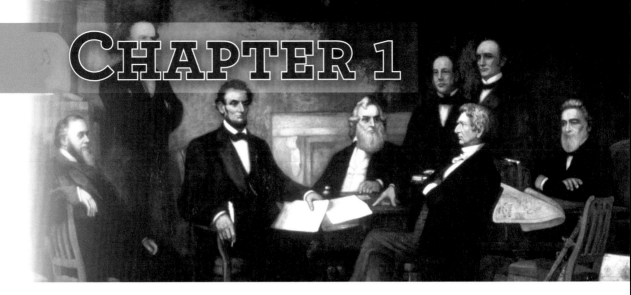

CHAPTER 1

PRELUDE TO WAR, 1850–60

Before the Civil War the United States experienced a whole generation of nearly unremitting political crisis. Underlying the problem was the fact that America in the early 19th century had been a country, not a nation. The major functions of government—those relating to education, transportation, health, and public order—were performed on the state or local level, and little more than a loose allegiance to the government in Washington, D.C., a few national institutions such as churches and political parties, and a shared memory of the Founding Fathers of the republic tied the country together. Within this loosely structured society every section, every state, every locality, and every group could mostly go its own way.

Gradually, however, changes in technology and in the economy were bringing all the elements of the country into steady and close contact. Improvements in transportation— first canals, then toll roads, and especially railroads—broke down isolation and encouraged the boy from the country to wander to the city, the farmer from New Hampshire to migrate to Iowa. Improvements in the printing press, which permitted the publication of penny newspapers, and the development of the telegraph system broke through the barriers of intellectual provincialism and made everybody almost instantaneously aware of what was going on throughout the country. As the railroad network proliferated, it had to have central direction and control; and national railroad corporations—the first true "big businesses" in the United States—emerged to provide order and stability.

For many Americans the wrench from a largely rural, slow-moving, fragmented society in the early 1800s to a bustling, integrated, national social order in the mid-century was an abrupt and painful one, and they often resisted it. Sometimes resentment against change manifested itself in harsh attacks upon those who appeared to be the agents of change—especially immigrants, who seemed to personify the forces that were altering the older America. Vigorous nativist movements appeared in most cities during the 1840s; but not until the 1850s, when the huge numbers of Irish and German immigrants of the previous decade became eligible to vote, did the antiforeign fever reach its peak. Directed both against immigrants and against the Roman Catholic church, to which so many of them belonged, the so-called Know-Nothings emerged as a powerful political force in 1854 and increased the resistance to change.

SECTIONALISM AND SLAVERY

A more enduring manifestation of hostility toward the nationalizing tendencies in American life was the reassertion of strong feelings of sectional loyalty. New Englanders felt threatened by the West, which drained off the ablest and most vigorous members of the labour force and, once the railroad network was complete, produced wool and grain that undersold the products of the poor New England hill country. The West, too, developed a strong sectional feeling, blending its sense of its uniqueness, its feeling of being looked down upon as raw and uncultured, and its awareness that it was being exploited by the businessmen of the East.

The most conspicuous and distinctive section, however, was the South—an area set apart by climate, by a plantation system designed for the production of such staple crops as cotton, tobacco, and sugar, and, especially, by the persistence of slavery, which had been abolished or prohibited in all other parts of the United States. It should not be thought, though, that all or even most white Southerners were directly involved in slavery. Indeed, in 1850 there were only 347,525 slaveholders in a total white population of about 6,000,000 in the slave states. Half of these owned four slaves or fewer and could not be considered planters. In the entire South there were fewer than 1,800 persons who owned more than 100 slaves.

Nevertheless, slavery did give a distinctive tone to the whole pattern of Southern life. If the large planters

Whitehall Street, Atlanta, Ga. A typical commercial street in the American South during the mid-19th century. The store in the centre sold furnishings and slaves. Universal Images Group/Hulton Archive/Getty Images

were few, they were also wealthy, prestigious, and powerful; often they were the political as well as the economic leaders of their section; and their values pervaded every stratum of Southern society. Far from opposing slavery, small farmers thought only of the possibility that they, too, might, with hard

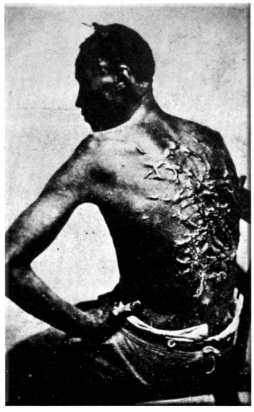

The inhumanity of slavery, as writ upon the back of an African American slave after a whipping. MPI/Archive Photos/Getty Images

work and good fortune, some day join the ranks of the planter class—to which they were closely connected by ties of blood, marriage, and friendship. Behind this virtually unanimous support of slavery lay the universal belief—shared by many whites in the North and West as well—that blacks were an innately inferior people who had risen only to a state of barbarism in their native Africa and who could live in a civilized society only if disciplined through slavery. Though by 1860 there were in fact about 250,000 free blacks in the South, most Southern whites resolutely refused to believe that the slaves, if freed, could ever coexist peacefully with their former masters. With shuddering horror, they pointed to an insurrection of blacks that had occurred in Santo Domingo, to a brief slave rebellion led by the African American Gabriel in Virginia in 1800, to a plot of Charleston, S.C., blacks headed by Denmark Vesey in 1822, and, especially, to a bloody and determined Virginia insurrection led by Nat Turner in 1831 as evidence that African Americans had to be kept under iron control. Facing increasing opposition to slavery outside their section, Southerners developed an elaborate proslavery argument, defending the institution on biblical, economic, and sociological grounds.

Slave Rebellions

The myth of the contented slave was essential to the preservation of the South's system of slavery, and the historical record of rebellions was frequently clouded by exaggeration, censorship, and distortion. Estimates of the total number of slave revolts vary according to the definition of insurrection. For the two centuries preceding the American Civil War (1861–65), one historian found documentary evidence of more than 250 uprisings or attempted uprisings involving 10 or more slaves whose aim was personal freedom. Few of these, however, were systematically planned, and most were merely spontaneous and quite short-lived disturbances by small groups of slaves. Such rebellions were usually attempted by male bondsmen and were often betrayed by house servants who identified more closely with their masters.

Three rebellions or attempted rebellions by slaves do deserve special notice, however. The first large-scale conspiracy was conceived in 1800 by Gabriel Prosser, a bondsman who is remembered today simply by his first name. On August 30 more than 1,000 armed slaves massed for action near Richmond, Va., but were thwarted by a violent rainstorm. The slaves were forced to disband, and 35 were hanged, including Gabriel. The only free person to lead a rebellion was Denmark Vesey, an urban artisan of Charleston, S.C. Vesey's rebellion (1822) was to have involved, according to some accounts, as many as 9,000 slaves from the surrounding area, but the conspiracy was betrayed in June before the plan could be effected. As a result 139 blacks were arrested, of whom 37 (including Vesey) were hanged and 32 exiled before the end of the summer. The third notable slave rebellion occurred in Southampton County, Va., in the summer of 1831 and was led by Nat Turner, a slave who learned to read from one of his master's sons and eagerly absorbed intensive religious training. In time his religious ardour tended to approach fanaticism, and he saw himself called upon by God to lead his people out of bondage. He began to exert a powerful influence on many of the nearby slaves, who called him "the Prophet." On the evening of August 21, Turner and seven other slaves started their crusade against bondage, killing a total of 57 whites and attracting up to 70 fellow slaves to the conspiracy during the next few days. On the 24th, hundreds of militia and volunteers stopped the rebels near Jerusalem, the county seat, killing at least 40 and probably nearer 100. Turner was hanged on November 11. As usual, a new wave of unrest spread through the South, accompanied by corresponding fear among slaveholders and passage of more repressive legislation directed against both slaves and free blacks. These measures were aimed particularly at restricting the education of blacks, their freedom of movement and assembly, and the circulation of inflammatory printed material.

Although the slave rebellion known as the Amistad mutiny occurred on a slave ship off the coast of Cuba in the summer of 1839, the 53 African captives who revolted were captured and tried in the United States after their ship entered U.S. waters. Their legal victory in 1840 in a federal court in Connecticut, a state in which slavery was legal, was upheld by the U.S. Supreme Court in the following year. With help from abolitionist and missionary groups, the Africans returned home to Sierra Leone in 1842.

In the decades preceding the American Civil War, increasing numbers of discontented slaves escaped to the North or to Canada via the Underground Railroad. Publicity in the North concerning black rebellions and the influx of fugitive slaves helped to arouse wider sympathy for the plight of the slave and support for the abolition movement.

A DECADE OF POLITICAL CRISES

In the early years of the republic, sectional differences had existed, but it had been possible to reconcile or ignore them because distances were great, communication was difficult, and the powerless national government had almost nothing to do. The revolution in transportation and communication, however, eliminated much of the isolation, and the victory of the United States in its brief war with Mexico left the national government with problems that required action.

POPULAR SOVEREIGNTY

The Compromise of 1850 was an uneasy patchwork of concessions to all sides that began to fall apart as soon as it was enacted. In the long run the principle of popular sovereignty—wherein the people of each territory would determine whether or not they would allow slavery within their boundaries—proved to be most unsatisfactory of all, as each territory became a battleground where the supporters of the South contended with the defenders of the North and West.

The seriousness of those conflicts became clear in 1854, when Sen. Stephen A. Douglas, a Democrat from Illinois who served as chairman of the Committee on Territories, introduced his Kansas bill in Congress, establishing a territorial government for the vast

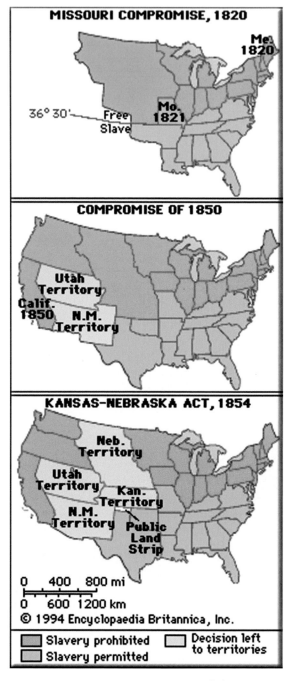

Compromises over extension of slavery into the territories.

region that lay between the Missouri River and the Rocky Mountains. In the Senate the bill was amended to create not one but two territories—Kansas and Nebraska—from the part of the Louisiana Purchase from which the Missouri Compromise of 1820 had forever excluded slavery.

Document: Stephen A. Douglas: Defense of the Kansas-Nebraska Act (1854)

Stephen Douglas's Kansas-Nebraska bill of 1854 was designed to allow the legislatures of Kansas and Nebraska to determine whether those territories should be slave or free. This plan, which in effect repealed the provisions of the Missouri Compromise (1820), was attacked by Douglas's fellow Democrats under the leadership of Ohio Sen. Salmon P. Chase. Douglas himself was so widely criticized that one Washington newspaper declared: "Never before has a public man been so hunted and bounded." In a speech of Jan. 30, 1854, Douglas defended the constitutionality of his bill and denounced Senator Chase and the antislavery faction for refusing to compromise on an issue that threatened to disrupt the Union. Portions of the speech are reprinted below.

Mr. President, when I proposed on Tuesday last that the Senate should proceed to the consideration of the bill to organize the territories of Nebraska and Kansas ... I desired to refer to two points: first, as to those provisions relating to the Indians; and second, to those which might be supposed to bear upon the question of slavery. ...

Sir, this is all that I intended to say if the question had been taken up for consideration on Tuesday last; but since that time occurrences have transpired which compel me to go more fully into the discussion. It will be borne in mind that the senator from Ohio [Mr. Chase] then objected to the consideration of the bill and asked for its postponement until this day, on the ground that there had not been time to understand and consider its provisions; and the senator from Massachusetts [Mr. Sumner] suggested that the postponement should be for one week, for that purpose. These suggestions seeming to be reasonable to senators around me, I yielded to their request and consented to the postponement of the bill until this day.

Sir, little did I suppose at the time that I granted that act of courtesy to those two senators that they had drafted and published to the world a document, over their own signatures, in which they arraigned me as having been guilty of a criminal betrayal of my trust, as having been guilty of an act of bad faith, and been engaged in an atrocious plot against the cause of free government. Little did I suppose that those two senators had been guilty of such conduct when they called upon me to grant that courtesy, to give them an opportunity of investigating the substitute reported from the committee.

I have since discovered that on that very morning the National Era, the Abolition organ in this city, contained an address, signed by certain Abolition confederates, to the people, in which the bill is grossly misrepresented, in which the action of the members of the committee is grossly falsified, in which our motives are arraigned and our characters calumniated....

Douglas, who was unconcerned over the moral issue of slavery and desirous of getting on with the settling of the West and the construction of a transcontinental railroad, knew that the Southern senators would block the organization of Kansas as a free territory. Recognizing that the North and West had outstripped their section in population and hence in the House of Representatives, Southerners clung desperately to an equality of votes in the Senate and were not disposed to welcome any new free territories, which would inevitably become additional free states (as California had done through the Compromise of 1850). Accordingly, Douglas thought that the doctrine of popular sovereignty, which had been applied to the territories gained from Mexico, would avoid a political contest over the Kansas territory: it would permit Southern slaveholders to move into the area, but, since the region was unsuited for plantation slavery, it would inevitably result in the formation of additional free states. His bill therefore allowed the inhabitants of the territory self-government in all matters of domestic importance, including the slavery issue. This provision in effect allowed the territorial legislatures to mandate slavery in their areas and was directly contrary to the Missouri Compromise. With the backing of President Franklin Pierce (served 1853–57), Douglas bullied, wheedled, and bluffed congressmen into passing his bill.

Polarization Over Slavery

Northern sensibilities were outraged by the passage of the Kansas-Nebraska Act. Although disliking slavery, Northerners had made few efforts to change the South's "peculiar institution" so long as the republic was loosely articulated. (Indeed, when prominent abolitionist William Lloyd Garrison began his *Liberator* in 1831, urging the immediate and unconditional emancipation of all slaves, he had only a tiny following; and a few years later he had actually been mobbed in Boston.) But with the sections, perforce, being drawn closely together, Northerners could no longer profess indifference to the South and its institutions. Sectional differences, centring on the issue of slavery, began to appear in every American institution. During the 1840s the major national religious denominations, such as the Methodists and the Presbyterians, split over the slavery question. The Whig Party, which had once allied the conservative businessmen of the North and West with the planters of the South, divided and virtually disappeared after the election of 1852. When Douglas's bill opened up to slavery Kansas and Nebraska—land that had long been reserved for the westward expansion of the free states—Northerners began to organize into an antislavery political party, called in some states the Anti-Nebraska Democratic Party, in others the People's Party, but in most places, the Republican Party.

An early meeting place for abolitionists, the Little White Schoolhouse in Ripon, Wis., is often called the birthplace of the Republican Party. MPI/Archive Photos/Getty Images

Events of 1855 and 1856 further exacerbated relations between the sections and strengthened this new party. Kansas, once organized by Congress, became the field of battle between the free and the slave states in a contest in which concern over slavery was mixed with land speculation and office

Document: Harriet Beecher Stowe's *Uncle Tom's Cabin,* Boston, 1883, pp. 419–423.

Few works of literature have had as immediate an impact upon the American political landscape as did Harriet Beecher Stowe's exposé of the inhumanity of slavery, Uncle Tom's Cabin. Stowe's heartrending tale, which was initially serialized in the abolitionist journal National Era (beginning in 1851), appeared in book form in 1852. An immediate success, it sold 300,000 copies during its first year and won much sympathy for the plight of slaves with its depiction of Uncle Tom, the first African American fictional hero created by an American author. In response to Southern denunciations of the book's authenticity, Stowe wrote a sequel, *A Key to Uncle Tom's Cabin* (1853), documenting the characters and events. Upon meeting Stowe, Abraham Lincoln may or may not have said, "So this is the little woman who wrote the book that started this great war"?

Long after dusk, the whole weary train, with their baskets on their heads, defiled up to the building appropriated to the storing and weighing the cotton. Legree was there, busily conversing with the two drivers . . . Slowly, the weary, dispirited creatures wound their way into the room, and, with crouching reluctance, presented their baskets to be weighed.

Legree noted on a slate, on the side of which was pasted a list of names,the amount.

Tom's basket was weighed and approved; and he looked, with an anxious glance, for the success of the woman he had befriended.

Tottering with weakness, she came forward and delivered her basket. It was of full weight, as Legree well perceived; but, affecting anger, he said, "What, you lazy beast! Short again! Stand aside, you'll catch it, pretty soon!"

The woman gave a groan of utter despair and sat down on a board.

The person who had been called Misse Cassy now came forward and, with a haughty, negligent air, delivered her basket. As she delivered it, Legree looked in her eyes with a sneering yet inquiring glance.

She fixed her black eyes steadily on him, her lips moved slightly, and she said something in French. What it was, no one knew, but Legree's face became perfectly demoniacal in its expression as she spoke; he half raised his hand as if to strike—a gesture which she regarded with fierce disdain as she turned and walked away.

"And now," said Legree, "come here, you Tom. You see I told ye I didn't buy ye jest for the common work; I mean to promote ye and make a driver of ye; and tonight ye may jest as well begin to get yer hand in. Now, ye jest take this yer gal and flog her; ye've seen enough on't to know how."

"I beg Mas'r's pardon," said Tom, "hopes Mas'r won't set me at that. It's what I an't used to—never did—and can't do, no way possible."

"Ye'll larn a pretty smart chance of things ye never did know before I've done with ye!" said Legree, taking up a cowhide and striking Tom a heavy blow across the cheek, and following up the infliction by a shower of blows.

"There!" he said, as he stopped to rest, "now will ye tell me ye can't do it?"

"Yes, Mas'r," said Tom, putting up his hand to wipe the blood that trickled down his face. "I'm willin' to work night and day, and work while there's life and breath in me; but this yer thing I can't feel it right to do; and, Mas'r, I never shall do it—never!"

Tom had a remarkably smooth, soft voice, and a habitually respectful manner that had given Legree an idea that he would be cowardly and easily subdued. When he spoke these last words, a thrill of amazement went through everyone; the poor woman clasped her hands and said, "O Lord!" and everyone involuntarily looked at each other and drew in their breath, as if to prepare for the storm that was about to burst.

seeking. A virtual civil war broke out, with rival free- and slave-state legislatures both claiming legitimacy. Disputes between individual settlers sometimes erupted into violence. A proslavery mob sacked the town of Lawrence, an antislavery stronghold, on May 21, 1856. On May 24–25 John Brown, a free-state partisan, led a small party in a raid upon some proslavery settlers on Pottawatomie Creek, murdered five men in cold blood, and left their gashed and mutilated bodies as a warning to the slaveholders.

Not even the U.S. Capitol was safe from the violence. On May 22 Preston S. Brooks, a South Carolina congressman, brutally attacked Sen. Charles Sumner of Massachusetts at his desk in the Senate chamber because he had presumably

Document: Charles Sumner: The Crime Against Kansas (1856)

As Kansas became a battleground for all the old animosities over the issue of slavery, Southerners claimed that under the principle of popular sovereignty Kansas would become "a den of Negro thieves and...incendiaries." In response to pro-slavery activity in Kansas, Sen. Charles Sumner delivered an attack on the slave interest in a speech before the Senate on May 19 and 20, 1856. That speech (reprinted here) evoked such strong emotion in Rep. Preston S. Brooks of South Carolina that two days later he entered the Senate chamber and gave Sumner a vicious beating with a cane, from which Sumner did not recover for several years.

Engraving showing the attack on Charles Sumner on the floor of the Senate, 1856; *from* Leslie's Illustrated Newspaper. Library of Congress, Washington, D.C.

It belongs to me now, in the first place, to expose the Crime Against Kansas in its origin and extent. Logically this is the beginning of the argument. I say crime, and deliberately adopt this strongest term as better than any other denoting the consummate transgression. I would go further if language could further go. It is the crime of crimes—surpassing far the old crimen majestatis [crime against a sovereign power], pursued with vengeance by the laws of Rome, and containing all other crimes, as the greater contains the less. I do not go too far when I call it the crime against nature, from which the soul recoils and which language refuses to describe. ...

Sir, the Nebraska Bill was in every respect a swindle. It was a swindle by the South of the North. It was, on the part of those who had already completely enjoyed their share of the Missouri Compromise, a swindle of those whose share was yet absolutely untouched; and the plea of unconstitutionality set up—like the plea of usury after the borrowed money has been enjoyed—did not make it less a swindle. Urged as a bill of peace, it was a swindle of the whole country. Urged as opening the doors to slave masters with their slaves, it was a swindle of the asserted doctrine of popular sovereignty. Urged as sanctioning popular sovereignty, it was a swindle of the asserted rights of slave masters. It was a swindle of a broad territory, thus cheated of protection against slavery. It was a swindle of a great cause, early espoused by Washington, Franklin, and Jefferson, surrounded by the best fathers of the republic. Sir, it was a swindle of God-given inalienable rights. Turn it over; look at it on all sides, and it is everywhere a swindle; and if the word I now employ has not the authority of classical usage, it has, on this occasion, the indubitable authority of fitness. No other word will adequately express the mingled meanness and wickedness of the cheat....

insulted the Carolinian's "honour" in a speech he had given in support of Kansas abolitionists.

The 1856 presidential election made it clear that voting was becoming polarized along sectional lines. Though James Buchanan, the Democratic nominee, was elected, John C. Frémont, the Republican candidate, received a majority of the votes in the free states.

Dred Scott

The following year the Supreme Court of the United States tried to solve the sectional conflicts that had baffled both the Congress and the president. Hearing

the case of Dred Scott, a Missouri slave who claimed freedom on the grounds that his master had taken him to live in free territory, the majority of the court, headed by Chief Justice Roger B. Taney, found that African Americans were not citizens of the United States and that Scott hence had no right to bring suit before the Court. Taney also concluded that the U.S. laws prohibiting slavery in the territory were unconstitutional. Two Northern antislavery judges on the court bitterly attacked Taney's logic and his conclusions. Acclaimed in the South, the *Dred Scott* decision was condemned and repudiated throughout the North.

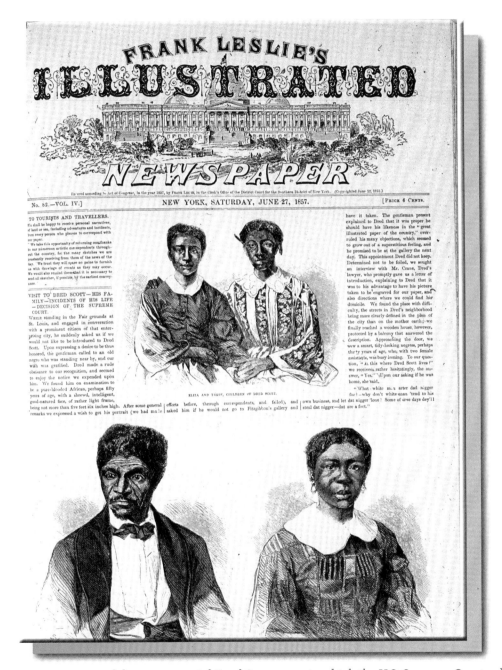

Front-page coverage of the controversial Dred Scott case, in which the U.S. Supreme Court ruled that Congress had no power to ban slavery in the territories and that slaves were not citizens.
MPI/Archive Photos/Getty Images

"THIS GOVERNMENT CANNOT ENDURE"

By this point many Americans, North and South, had come to the conclusion that slavery and freedom could not much longer coexist in the United States. For Southerners the answer was withdrawal from a Union that no longer protected their rights and interests; they had talked of it as early as the Nashville Convention of 1850, when the compromise measures

Document: Roger B. Taney: *Dred Scott* v. *Sandford* (1857)

By the mid-1850s there existed a widespread feeling that the slavery question, which Congress had been unable to resolve, should be dealt with by the courts; and Pres. James Buchanan, in his inaugural address (March 4, 1857), made reference to a coming decision that he hoped all would be able to abide by. Two days later, on March 6, the Supreme Court handed down its ruling in Dred Scott v. Sandford, a case as famous as any in its history. Dred Scott, a slave of mixed parentage, had been taken by his master to Illinois, where slavery had been forbidden by the Ordinance of 1787, and to the Wisconsin Territory, which also did not allow slavery. Scott had remained on free soil during most of the period from 1834 to 1838. In 1846 he had sued for his liberty in a Missouri court, holding that he had become free because of his stay in free territory. The case involved three important issues: (1) whether Scott was a citizen of Missouri and thus able to sue in a federal court; (2) whether his sojourn in free territory had made him legally a free man; and (3) the constitutionality of the Missouri Compromise. Each of the judges handed down a separate opinion, although that of Chief Justice Roger Taney is customarily cited for the majority. In effect, the majority ruling held that Scott (and hence all slaves or their descendants) was not a citizen; that his status in free territory did not affect his status in Missouri, where slavery was legal; and that the Missouri Compromise was unconstitutional under the Fifth Amendment. The decision was eventually nullified by the Thirteenth and Fourteenth Amendments.

Mr. Chief Justice Taney delivered the opinion of the Court....

The question is simply this: Can a Negro, whose ancestors were imported into this country and sold as slaves, become a member of the political community formed and brought into existence by the Constitution of the United States, and as such become entitled to all the rights and privileges and immunities, guaranteed by that instrument to the citizen? One of which rights is the privilege of suing in a court of the United States in the cases specified in the Constitution.

It will be observed that the plea applies to that class of persons only whose ancestors were Negroes of the African race and imported into this country, and sold and held as slaves. The only matter in issue before the Court, therefore, is whether the descendants of such slaves, when they shall be emancipated, or who are born of parents who had become free before their birth, are citizens of a state in the sense in which the word "citizen" is used in the Constitution of the United States. And this being the only matter in dispute on the pleadings, the Court must be understood as speaking in this opinion of that class only; that is, of those persons who are the descendants of Africans who were imported into this country and sold as slaves....

were under consideration, and now more and more Southerners favoured secession. For Northerners the remedy was to change the social institutions of the South; few advocated immediate or complete emancipation of the slaves, but many felt that the South's slave system had to be contained.

In 1858 William H. Seward, the leading Republican of New York, spoke of an "irrepressible conflict" between freedom and slavery; and in Illinois a rising Republican politician, Abraham Lincoln, announced that "this government cannot endure, permanently half *slave* and half *free*."

Abraham Lincoln. SuperStock/Getty Images

Document: Abraham Lincoln: "A House Divided" (1858)

The speech by Abraham Lincoln to the Republican State Convention in Springfield, Ill., on June 16, 1858, launched his campaign for the U.S. Senate seat held by Stephen A. Douglas. Douglas replied less than a month later in Chicago, after which the two men sparred in their famous series of debates. Lincoln's speech was considered radical at the time and potentially dangerous. His former law partner, William H. Herndon, predicted, however, that the Republicans would eventually make him president.

Mr. President and Gentlemen of the Convention:

If we could first know where we are and whither we are tending, we could better judge what to do and how to do it. We are now far into the fifth year since a policy was initiated with the avowed object and confident promise of putting an end to slavery agitation. Under the operation of that policy, that agitation has not only not ceased but has constantly augmented. In my opinion, it will not cease until a crisis shall have been reached and passed. "A house divided against itself cannot stand." I believe this government cannot endure, permanently, half slave and half free. I do not expect the Union to be dissolved; I do not expect the house to fall; but I do expect it will cease to be divided. It will become all one thing, or all the other. Either the opponents of slavery will arrest the further spread of it and place it where the public mind shall rest in the belief that it is in the course of ultimate extinction, or its advocates will push it forward till it shall become alike lawful in all the states, old as well as new, North as well as South.

Have we no tendency to the latter condition?

Let anyone who doubts carefully contemplate that now almost complete legal combination—piece of machinery, so to speak—compounded of the Nebraska doctrine and the Dred Scott decision. Let him consider, not only what work the machinery is adapted to do, and how well adapted, but also let him study the history of its construction and trace, if he can, or rather fail, if he can, to trace the evidences of design and concert of action among its chief architects, from the beginning....

RAID ON HARPERS FERRY

That it was not possible to end the agitation over slavery became further apparent in 1859, when on the night of October 16, John Brown, who had escaped punishment for the Pottawatomie massacre, staged a raid on Harpers Ferry, Va. (now in W. Va.), designed to free the slaves and, apparently, to help them begin a guerrilla war against the Southern whites. Even though Brown was promptly captured and Virginia slaves gave no heed to his appeals, Southerners feared that this was the beginning of organized Northern efforts to undermine their social system. The fact that Brown was a fanatic and an inept strategist whose actions were considered questionable

View of the town of Harpers Ferry, Va. (now in West Virginia), and railroad bridge. Library of Congress, Washington, D.C. (LC-B8171-7187 DLC)

even by many abolitionists did not lessen Northern admiration for him.

A NEW PRESIDENT

The presidential election of 1860 occurred, therefore, in an atmosphere of great tension. Southerners, determined that their rights should be guaranteed by law, insisted upon a Democratic candidate willing to protect slavery in the territories; and they rejected Stephen A. Douglas, whose popular-sovereignty doctrine left the question in doubt, in favour of John C. Breckinridge. Douglas, backed by most of the Northern and border-state Democrats, ran on a separate Democratic ticket. Elderly conservatives, who deplored all agitation of the sectional questions but advanced no solutions, offered John Bell as candidate of the Constitutional Union Party. Republicans, confident of success, passed over the claims of Seward, who had accumulated too many liabilities in his long public career, and

Document: Henry David Thoreau: A Plea for Captain John Brown (1859)

John Brown, whose career in Kansas had led some to think him a madman, conceived a quixotic plan in 1859 whereby he hoped to bring about a general slave uprising in the South. On October 16 he led a group of about 20 men in a raid on the federal arsenal at Harpers Ferry, in the hope of obtaining weapons with which to arm the slaves. Much to his surprise, very few African Americans showed interest in Brown's scheme. Sporadic fighting occurred for two days around the arsenal. On October 18, a detachment of one hundred marines commanded by Col. Robert E. Lee and including Lieut. J. E. B. Stuart subdued Brown and his men. Brown was indicted for treason on October 25. Five days later essayist and philosopher Henry David Thoreau became the first man to champion Brown publicly, delivering the following speech to his protesting fellow townsmen. A month later, when he heard that Brown had been executed, Thoreau said: "I heard, to be sure, that he had been hanged, but I did not know what that meant—and not after any number of days shall I believe it. Of all the men who are said to be my contemporaries, it seems to me that John Brown is the only one who has not died."

I trust that you will pardon me for being here. I do not wish to force my thoughts upon you, but I feel forced myself. Little as I know of Captain Brown, I would fain do my part to correct the tone and the statements of the newspapers, and of my countrymen generally, respecting his character and actions. It costs us nothing to be just. We can at least express our sympathy with and admiration of him and his companions, and that is what I now propose to do. ...

When the troubles in Kansas began, he sent several of his sons thither to strengthen the party of the free state men, fitting them out with such weapons as he had; telling them that if the troubles should increase and there should be need of him, he would follow to assist them with his hand and counsel. This, as you all know, he soon after did; and it was through his agency, far more than any other's, that Kansas was made free. ...

I should say that he was an old-fashioned man in his respect for the Constitution and his faith in the permanence of this Union. Slavery he deemed to be wholly opposed to these, and he was its determined foe....

nominated Lincoln instead. Voting in the subsequent election was along markedly sectional patterns, with Republican strength confined almost completely to the North and West. Though Lincoln received only a plurality of the popular vote, he was an easy winner in the electoral college.

CHAPTER 2

SECESSION AND THE POLITICS OF THE CIVIL WAR, 1860–65

In the South, Lincoln's election was taken as the signal for secession, and on December 20 South Carolina became the first state to withdraw from the Union. Promptly the other states of the lower South followed. Feeble efforts on the part of Buchanan's administration to check secession failed, and one by one most of the federal forts in the Southern states were taken over by secessionists. Meanwhile, strenuous efforts in Washington to work out another compromise failed. The most promising plan was the proposal of John J. Crittenden of Kentucky.

Crittenden envisioned six constitutional amendments by which the Missouri Compromise of 1820 was, in effect, to be reenacted and, more important, to be extended to the Pacific; the federal government was to indemnify owners of fugitive slaves whose return was prevented by antislavery elements in the North; "squatter sovereignty" (the right to decide if slavery should exist or not) in the territories was to be sanctioned; and slavery in the District of Columbia was to be protected from congressional action. On March 2, 1861, Crittenden's plan was narrowly defeated in the Senate. Two

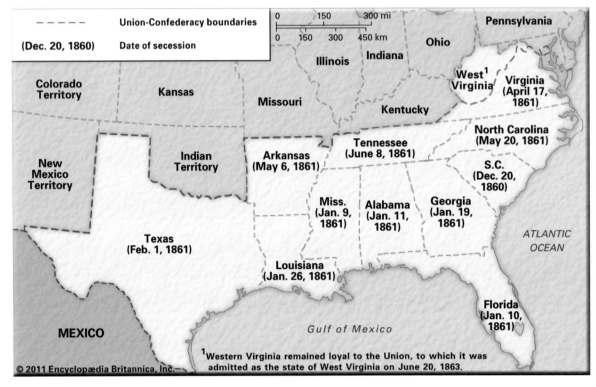

Dates of secession by Southern states. Encyclopædia Britannica, Inc.

months earlier, he had introduced a resolution calling for a national referendum on these proposals, but the Senate never acted on this resolution.

THE COMING OF WAR

Neither extreme Southerners, now intent upon secession, nor Republicans, intent upon reaping the rewards of their hard-won election victory, were really interested in compromise. On Feb. 4, 1861—a month before Lincoln could be inaugurated in Washington—six Southern states (South Carolina, Georgia, Alabama, Florida, Mississippi, and Louisiana) sent representatives to Montgomery, Ala., to set up a new independent government. Delegates from Texas soon joined them. With Jefferson Davis of Mississippi at its head, the Confederate States of America came into being, set up its own bureaus and offices, issued its own money, raised its own taxes, and flew its own flag. Not until May 1861, after hostilities had broken out and Virginia had seceded, did the new government transfer its capital to Richmond.

Document: Henry Timrod: "Ethnogenesis" (1861)

Henry Timrod was unrecognized as a poet until the Southern secession and the Civil War. The emotions that stirred the South in 1860–61 led to a flowering of his poetic talents, and by the time the Confederacy was formed he was regarded as the South's poet laureate. "Ethnogenesis" was written.while Timrod was attending the First Southern Congress, in Montgomery, Ala., in February 1861. Originally entitled Ode, on the Meeting of the Southern Congress, it was first printed in the Charleston Mercury on September 26. In the poem (reprinted here, beginning with its first stanza) Timrod eloquently sings of the birth of the new nation, expresses the patriotic spirit of his country-men, and presents his ideas of the South's mission and of the Southern character.

> *Hath not the morning dawned with added light?*
> *And shall not evening call another star*
> *Out of the infinite regions of the night,*
> *To mark this day in Heaven? At last, we are*
> *A nation among nations; and the world*
> *Shall soon behold in many a distant port*
> *Another flag unfurled!*
> *Now, come what may, whose favor need we court?*
> *And, under God, whose thunder need we fear?*
> *Thank Him who placed us here*
> *Beneath so kind a sky — the very sun*
> *Takes part with us; and on our errands run*
> *All breezes of the ocean; dew and rain*
> *Do noiseless battle for us; and the year,*
> *And all the gentle daughters in her train,*
> *March in our ranks, and in our service wield*
> *Long spears of golden grain!*
> *A yellow blossom as her fairy shield,*
> *June flings her azure banner to the wind,*
> *While in the order of their birth*
> *Her sisters pass, and many an ample field*
> *Grows white beneath their steps, till now, behold,*
> *Its endless sheets unfold*
> *The snow of Southern summers! Let the earth*
> *Rejoice! beneath those fleeces soft and warm*
> *Our happy land shall sleep*
> *In a repose as deep*
> *As if we lay entrenched behind*
> *Whole leagues of Russian ice and Arctic storm!...*

THE FIRST SHOT IS FIRED

Faced with a fait accompli, Lincoln when inaugurated was prepared to conciliate the South in every way but one: he would not recognize that the Union could be divided. The test of his determination came early in his administration, when he learned that the federal troops under Major Robert Anderson in Fort Sumter, S.C.—then one of the few military installations in the South still in federal hands—had to be promptly supplied or withdrawn. After agonized consultation with his cabinet, Lincoln determined that supplies must be sent even if doing so provoked the Confederates into firing the first shot. On April 12, 1861, just before federal supply ships could reach the beleaguered Anderson, Confederate guns in Charleston opened fire upon Fort Sumter, and the war began.

Fort Sumter, a symbolic outpost of Union authority near Charleston, S.C., in the heart of the emergent Confederacy, is seen here bombarded by onshore batteries in the first battle of the American Civil War. Library of Congress Prints and Photographs Division

THE POLITICAL COURSE OF THE WAR

For the next four years, from 1861 to 1865, the Union and the Confederacy were locked in conflict—by far the most titanic waged in the Western Hemisphere.

The policies pursued by the governments of Abraham Lincoln and Jefferson Davis were astonishingly similar. Both

Document: Abraham Lincoln: First Inaugural Address (1861)

Abraham Lincoln wrote the first draft of his first inaugural address in Springfield, Ill., in January 1861. According to William H. Herndon, Lincoln's biographer and former law partner, he used only a handful of sources, among them Kentucky politician Henry Clay's famous speech of 1850, the U.S. Constitution, and Andrew Jackson's Proclamation Regarding Nullification. Lincoln reworked

The inauguration of Abraham Lincoln as U.S. president, Washington, D.C., March 4, 1861. Library of Congress Prints and Photographs Division

the speech countless times, always with an eye toward expressing a more conciliatory position. In referring to Southern secession, he changed "treasonable" to "revolutionary." His first draft ended on a warlike note: "You can forbear the assault upon it [the government]; I cannot shrink from the defense of it. With you, and not with me, is the solemn question of 'Shall it be peace, or a sword?'" On Secretary of State William H. Seward's advice, he substituted a sentimental appeal to his country-men's pride in their common heritage. During the days preceding the inauguration, the capital was rife with rumours of violence and assassination. Tension mounted as thousands of soldiers took their places in and around the Capitol. On March 4, ten thousand people heard the president, an unusu-ally small gathering owing to the widespread fear of violence. The address evoked some applause but little enthusiasm. But in the week that followed, wrote Carl Sandburg in his biography of Lincoln, "[the address] was the most widely read and closely scrutinized utterance that had ever come from an American President." The political positions had indeed hardened. Many Southern editorials asserted that the address was an act of war, while Northern papers saw it as a peace offering.

In compliance with a custom as old as the government itself, I appear before you to address you briefly and to take, in your presence, the oath prescribed by the Constitution of the United States to be taken by the President "before he enters on the execution of his office."

I do not consider it necessary, at present, for me to discuss those matters of administration about which there is no special anxiety or excitement. Apprehension seems to exist among the people of the Southern states that, by the accession of a Republican administration, their property and their peace and personal security are to be endangered. There has never been any reasonable cause for such apprehension. Indeed, the most ample evidence to the contrary has all the while existed and been open to their inspection. It is found in nearly all the published speeches of him who now addresses you.

I do but quote from one of those speeches when I declare that "I have no purpose, directly or indirectly, to interfere with the institution of slavery in the states where it exists. I believe I have no lawful right to do so, and I have no inclination to do so." Those who nominated and elected me did so with full knowledge that I had made this and many similar declarations, and had never recanted them. And, more than this, they placed in the platform, for my acceptance; and as a law to them-selves and to me, the clear and emphatic resolution which I now read:...

presidents at first relied upon volunteers to man the armies, and both administra-tions were poorly prepared to arm and equip the hordes of young men who flocked to the colours in the initial stages of the war. As the fighting progressed, both governments reluctantly resorted to conscription—the Confederates first, in early 1862, and the federal government more slowly, with an ineffective measure of late 1862 followed by a more stringent law in 1863. Both governments pur-sued an essentially laissez-faire policy in economic matters, with little effort to control prices, wages, or profits. Only the railroads were subject to close gov-ernment regulation in both regions; and the Confederacy, in constructing some of its own powder mills, made a few experiments in "state socialism." Neither Lincoln's nor Davis's administration knew how to cope with financing the war; neither developed an effective system of taxation until late in the conflict, and both relied heavily upon borrowing. Faced with a shortage of funds, both governments were obliged to turn to the printing press and to issue fiat money—that is, notes that are issued on the fiat (official endorsement) of the sovereign government, are specified to have a certain worth, and are legal tender but are not promises to pay something else. The U.S. government issued $432,000,000 in "greenbacks" (as this irredeemable, non-interest-bearing paper money was called), while the Confederacy printed over $1,554,000,000 in such paper currency. In consequence, both sections experienced runaway inflation, which was much more drastic in the South, where, by the end of the war, flour sold at $1,000 a barrel.

Even toward slavery, the root cause of the war, the policies of the two warring governments were surprisingly similar. The Confederate constitution, which was in most other ways similar to that of the United States, expressly guaranteed the institution of slavery. Despite pressure from abolitionists, Lincoln's administration was not initially disposed to disturb the slave system if only because any move toward emancipation would upset the loyalty of Delaware, Maryland, Kentucky, and Missouri—the four slave states that remained in the Union.

MOVES TOWARD EMANCIPATION

Gradually, however, under the pressure of war, both governments moved to end slavery. Lincoln came to see that

Document: John S. Rock: African American Hopes for Emancipation (1862)

Many African Americans saw in the Civil War the promise of emancipation. One of the most prominent African American leaders was Dr. John S. Rock, a Boston physician and attorney and the first African American lawyer admitted to the bar of the U.S. Supreme Court. He was one of the few leaders who looked beyond the immediate issues of the war to ask what would become of free African Americans in a white society. In a speech delivered in 1858 he sought to answer his own question. "When the avenues to wealth are opened to us," he declared, "we will then become educated and wealthy, and then the roughest looking colored man that you ever saw...will be pleasanter than the harmonies of Orpheus, and black will be a very pretty color." The speech reprinted below was given on Jan. 23, 1862, before the Massachusetts Anti-Slavery Society.

Ladies and Gentlemen:

I am here not so much to make a speech as to add a little more color to this occasion.

I do not know that it is right that I should speak at this time, for it is said that we have talked too much already; and it is being continually thundered in our ears that the time for speechmaking has

ended, and the time for action has arrived. Perhaps this is so. This may be the theory of the people, but we all know that the active idea has found but little sympathy with either of our great military commanders or the national executive; for they have told us, again and again, that "patience is a cure for all sores," and that we must wait for the "good time," which, to us, has been long a-coming.

It is not my desire, neither is it the time for me, to criticize the government, even if I had the disposition so to do. The situation of the black man in this country is far from being an enviable one. Today, our heads are in the lion's mouth, and we must get them out the best way we can. To contend against the government is as difficult as it is to sit in Rome and fight with the pope. It is probable that, if we had the malice of the Anglo-Saxon, we would watch our chances and seize the first opportunity to take our revenge. If we attempted this, the odds would be against us, and the first thing we should know would be—nothing! The most of us are capable of perceiving that the man who spits against the wind spits in his own face!...

emancipation of African Americans would favourably influence European opinion toward the Northern cause, might deprive the Confederates of their productive labour force on the farms, and would add much-needed recruits to the federal armies.

Secretary of State Seward had advised Lincoln that he should postpone the proclamation until the Union had achieved some military success, otherwise "it may be viewed as the last measure of an exhausted government, a cry for help." Heeding this advice, Lincoln waited until after the decisive Battle of Antietam (September 17) stopped Lee's advance upon Washington to issue his preliminary proclamation of emancipation, promising to free all slaves in rebel territory by Jan. 1, 1863, unless those states returned to the Union; and when the Confederates remained obdurate, he followed it with his promised final proclamation. A natural accompaniment of emancipation was the use of African American troops, and by the end of the war the number of blacks who served in the

federal armies totaled 178,895. Uncertain of the constitutionality of his Emancipation Proclamation, Lincoln urged Congress to abolish slavery by constitutional amendment; but this was not done until Jan. 31, 1865, with the Thirteenth Amendment, and the actual ratification did not take place until after the war.

Meanwhile the Confederacy, though much more slowly, was also inexorably drifting in the direction of emancipation. The South's desperate need for troops caused many military men, including Robert E. Lee, to demand the recruitment of blacks; finally, in March 1865 the Confederate congress authorized the raising of African American regiments. Though a few blacks were recruited for the Confederate armies, none actually served in battle because surrender was at hand. In yet another way Davis's government showed its awareness of slavery's inevitable end when, in a belated diplomatic mission to seek assistance from Europe, the Confederacy in March 1865 promised

Abraham Lincoln: Emancipation Proclamation (1863)

In the popular mind the Emancipation Proclamation transformed the Civil War from a struggle to preserve the Union into a crusade for human freedom. But at the time of its issuance, its actual provisions had already largely been enacted into law by Congress, which had provided for the freeing of slaves of owners hostile to the Union, the prohibition of slavery in the District of Columbia and the territories, and the freeing of slave-soldiers. The Emancipation Proclamation actually did not free a single slave, since the regions in which it authorized emancipation were under Confederate control, and in the border states where emancipation might have been effected, it was not authorized. It did, however, tremendously boost Union morale, breed disaffection in the South, and bolster support for the Union cause in Europe. The real significance of the document lay in the political factors that brought it to fruition and in the delicate political balance it preserved. By the summer of 1862, Lincoln had exhausted all other schemes short of full emancipation. African Americans in the North had objected to his offer of colonization; the border states disapproved of his proposal of compensated emancipation; and abolitionists were demanding a more radical course. The military position of the North had deteriorated when on July 22, 1862, Lincoln called together his cabinet to discuss emancipation. The president later described this fateful day in a conversation with the painter Frank Carpenter. "Things had gone on

Abraham Lincoln called the Emancipation Proclamation "the central act of my administration, and the greatest event of the 19th century." General Records of the U.S. Government, National Archives, Washington, D.C.

from bad to worse," said Lincoln, "until I felt that we had reached the end of our rope.... We had about played our last card, and must change our tactics, or lose the game!" Lincoln had prepared a draft of the proclamation prior to the cabinet meeting, "without consultation with or the knowledge of the cabinet." The majority of the cabinet were enthusiastic, including Secretary of State Seward, who raised, however, an objection to its timing. Ultimately, the Emancipation Proclamation as reprinted here, was issued on Jan. 1, 1863.

Whereas, on the 22nd day of September, in the year of our Lord 1862, a proclamation was issued by the President of the United States, containing, among other things, the following, to wit:

That on the 1st day of January, in the year of our Lord 1863, all persons held as slaves within any state or designated part of a state, the people whereof shall then be in rebellion against the United States, shall be then, thenceforward, and forever free; and the executive government of the

United States, including the military and naval authority thereof, will recognize and maintain the freedom of such persons and will do no act or acts to repress such persons, or any of them, in any efforts they may make for their actual freedom.

That the executive will, on the 1st day of January aforesaid, by proclamation, designate the states and parts of states, if any, in which the people thereof, respectively, shall then be in rebellion against the United States; and the fact that any state or the people thereof shall on that day be in good faith represented in the Congress of the United States by members chosen thereto at elections wherein a majority of the qualified voters of such states shall have participated shall, in the absence of strong countervailing testimony, be deemed conclusive evidence that such state and the people thereof are not then in rebellion against the United States....

to emancipate the slaves in return for diplomatic recognition. Nothing came of the proposal, but it is further evidence that by the end of the war both North and South realized that slavery was doomed.

SECTIONAL DISSATISFACTION

As war leaders, both Lincoln and Davis came under severe attack in their own sections. Both had to face problems of disloyalty. In order to wage war, both presidents had to strengthen the powers of central government, thus further accelerating the process of national integration that had brought on the war. Both administrations were, in consequence, vigorously attacked by state governors, who resented the encroachment upon their authority and who strongly favoured local autonomy.

So threatening were the divisions in the North to the war's conduct that Lincoln referred to dissent on the home front as "the fire in the rear." A large subset of the Democratic Party was adamantly opposed to the war. The politicians among these self-proclaimed Peace Democrats tended to represent the Midwest, especially Ohio, Indiana, and Illinois, where many families had Southern roots and where the agrarian way of life still held sway. They resented the growing dominance of industrialists in the Republican Party and the federal government, they disliked the railroad's shift of commerce toward the East, and they had special contempt for New England. Republicans, in turn, saw the Peace Democrats' opposition to the war as treasonous and labeled them Copperheads, a name derived from that of a stealthy, poisonous snake common to the American wilderness.

The Copperheads wanted not just to negotiate peace and bring the Confederacy back into the fold; they wanted to return to an earlier America. "The Constitution as it is, the Union as it was" was their rallying cry. They resented Lincoln's revocation of the writ of habeas corpus, done largely in response to the Copperheads' efforts to discourage enlistment and support deserters. They called Lincoln a tyrant and accused him of muzzling the press, though prominent newspapers in the North continued

Mob lynching of a black man in New York City during the Draft Riot of 1863. Fotosearch/Archive Photos/Getty Images

to take strong antiwar stands. And the Copperheads repeatedly bemoaned the war's cost in blood and treasure.

Above all the Copperheads opposed emancipation. They nakedly exploited Northern racism and white labourers' fear that their jobs would be taken by freed slaves willing to work for lower wages. They inveighed against a war that the Copperheads claimed was being fought for blacks but that would reduce whites' standard of living. Among those who responded most strongly to this message were immigrant groups, especially Irish Catholics in the Northeast, who were keenly fearful of losing their livelihood.

The introduction of conscription in 1863 gave the Copperheads a new slogan: "Rich man's war, poor man's fight." The law allowed a draftee to pay someone to take his place. It also permitted draftees to pay $300 for exemption from service. However, this commutation fee was seen as beyond the means of most working men. "Three Hundred dollars or your life" read the headlines in Democratic newspapers. In July 1863, as Union and Confederate forces clashed at Gettysburg, the rhetoric and rage that swelled on the home front erupted in four days of violence in New York City that became known as the Draft Riot of 1863. After burning draft offices

Document: Clement A. Vallandigham: A Plea to Stop the War (1863)

Clement Vallandigham, an Ohio lawyer and congressman, became the most famous of the Copperheads. His roots in Virginia inspired him with a devotion to the South, but far stronger was his devotion to the cause of peace. In a speech at Cooper Union in New York City on Nov. 2, 1860, Vallandigham asserted he would never "as a Representative in the Congress of the United States, vote one dollar of money whereby one drop of American blood should be shed in a civil war." Throughout the war years he made speeches in the North against the war and the administration. Republicans branded him a traitor, while many war-weary Northerners extolled him as an apostle of freedom. The following speech, given before the Democratic Union Association in New York City on March 7, 1863, was one of several that led to his arrest for treason on May 5, 1863. Lincoln subsequently banished him to the Confederacy. From there, Vallandigham escaped to Canada and then returned to the North. He continued to argue for peace at any cost, a message that hindered Democratic chances during the 1864 election.

The men who are in power at Washington, extending their agencies out through the cities and states of the Union and threatening to reinaugurate a reign of terror, may as well know that we comprehend precisely their purpose. I beg leave to assure you that it cannot and will not be permitted to succeed. The people of this country endorsed it once because they were told that it was essential to "the speedy suppression or crushing out of the rebellion" and the restoration of the Union; and they so loved the Union of these states that they would consent, even for a little while, under the false and now broken promises of the men in power, to surrender those liberties in order that the great object might, as was promised, be accomplished speedily.

They have been deceived; instead of crushing out the rebellion, the effort has been to crush out the spirit of liberty. The conspiracy of those in power is not so much for a vigorous prosecution of the war against rebels in the South as against the democracy in peace at home....

and attacking police, rioters, many of them immigrants, turned upon innocent African Americans, their property, and their institutions. Union troops had to be recalled from the battlefront to quell the violence.

PRESIDENTIAL ELECTION OF 1864

The war dragged on as the 1864 presidential election approached. Lincoln worried that he would not be reelected and that his crusade would crumble. He faced criticism on all sides.

Radical Republicans scorned the president's plans for Reconstruction and thought that he was moving too slowly toward abolishing slavery. They encouraged the candidacy of Secretary of the Treasury Salmon P. Chase, a member of the "Team of Rivals," a name

Pres. Abraham Lincoln and Gen. George B. McClellan in the general's tent, Antietam, Md. October 3, 1862. Photograph by Alexander Gardner. Library of Congress, Washington, D.C. (LC-B8171-0602 DLC)

historian Doris Kearns Goodwin applied to the political titans Lincoln had brought together in his cabinet. Many of them had run against Lincoln for the 1860 nomination. Chase still harboured that ambition but ultimately demurred when Lincoln's partisans skillfully rallied in support of him. Some Republicans then briefly backed John C. Frémont, the party's candidate in the 1856 presidential election, now a Union general without a high-profile command.

Lincoln's biggest challenge, however, came from another frustrated general, George B. McClellan, whom Lincoln had removed as the commander of the Army of the Potomac in 1862. As a War Democrat, McClellan supported continuing the fight but opposed emancipation. Still, McClellan became the presidential candidate for a Democratic Party whose platform was firmly grounded in Copperhead policy.

It was widely believed that the votes of Union soldiers would determine the election's outcome. Would their loyalty lie with "Father Abraham" or with their old general? In the event, the military vote was less crucial than had been believed. Before the election the Union's fortunes in war improved dramatically, most notably with William Tecumseh Sherman's capture of Atlanta. Support for Lincoln ballooned, and he was reelected with 55 percent of the popular vote.

Residents of the Southern hill country, where slavery never had much of a foothold, were similarly hostile toward Davis. In the Confederacy the congressional elections of 1863 went so strongly against the administration that Davis was able to command a majority for his measures only through the continued support of representatives and senators from the states of the upper South, which were under control of the federal army and consequently unable to hold new elections. In the last years of the war, Davis was openly attacked by Alexander H. Stephens, the vice president of the Confederacy. With each successive military defeat, Davis's administration lost support. In January 1865 the Confederate congress insisted that Davis make Robert E. Lee the supreme commander of all Southern forces. (Some, it is clear, would have preferred to make Lee the general dictator.)

CHAPTER 3

THE CIVIL WAR

FIGHTING THE WAR

Following the capture of Fort Sumter, both sides quickly began raising and organizing armies. On July 21, 1861, some 30,000 Union troops marching toward the Confederate capital of Richmond, Va., were stopped at Bull Run (Manassas) and then driven back to Washington, D.C., by Confederates under Gen. Thomas J. "Stonewall" Jackson and Gen. P.G.T. Beauregard. The shock of defeat galvanized the Union, which called for 500,000 more recruits. Gen. George B. McClellan was given the job of training the Union's Army of the Potomac. The first major campaign of the war began in February 1862, when the Union general Ulysses S. Grant captured the Confederate strongholds of Fort Henry and Fort Donelson in western Tennessee; this action was followed by the Union general John Pope's capture of New Madrid, Mo.

The Confederates had acknowledged the importance of Fort Henry and Fort Donelson by abandoning their strong position at Columbus, Ky., and by evacuating Nashville.

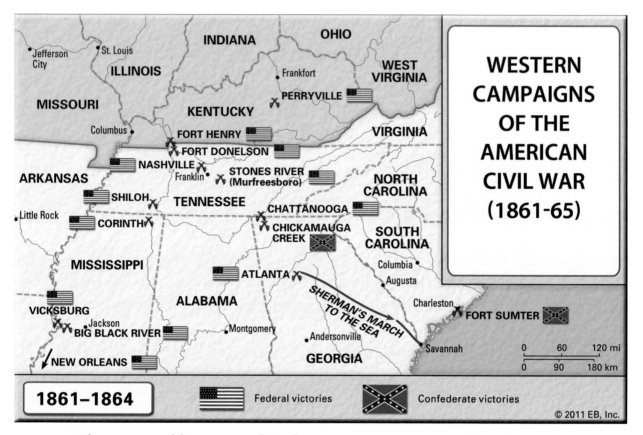

The main area of the western and Carolinas campaigns, 1861–65. Encyclopædia Britannica, Inc.

Grant's next aim was to attack the Memphis and Charleston Railroad, and to this end he encamped his troops on the Tennessee at Pittsburg Landing. At this point Gen. A.S. Johnston, commanding Confederate forces in the West, and General Beauregard were collecting a force aimed at recovering some of their recent losses. Since Union troops were planning an offensive, they had not fortified their camps. On April 6, to their surprise, General Johnston seized the initiative and attacked Grant before reinforcements could arrive. The Battle of Shiloh (also known as the Battle of Pittsburg Landing) was fought in the woods by inexperienced troops on both sides. Johnston was mortally wounded on the first afternoon. Despite a rallying of Northern troops and reinforcements for the South, the battle ended the next day with the Union army doing little more than reoccupying the camp it had lost the day before while the Confederates returned to Corinth, Miss. Although both sides claimed victory, it was a Confederate failure; both sides were immobilized for the next three weeks because of the heavy casualties—about 10,000 men on each side.

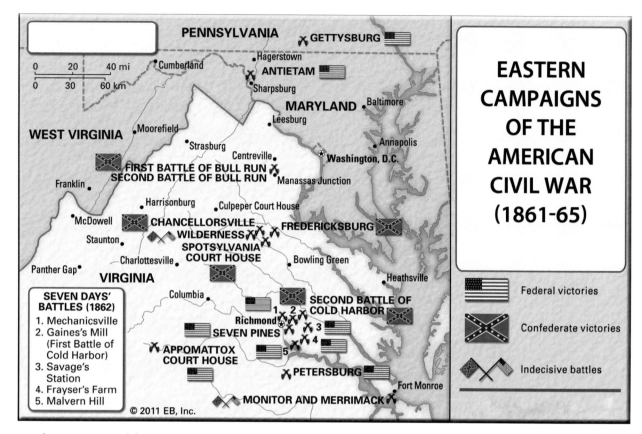

The main area of the eastern campaigns, 1861–65. Encyclopædia Britannica, Inc.

BLOODY BATTLES AND HEAVY CASUALTIES

Also in April 1862, the Union naval commodore David G. Farragut gained control of New Orleans. In the East, McClellan launched a long-awaited offensive with 100,000 men in another attempt to capture Richmond. Opposed by Gen. Robert E. Lee and his able lieutenants Jackson and J.E. Johnston, McClellan moved cautiously and in the Seven Days' Battles (June 25–July 1) was turned back.

After the indecisive Battle of Oak Grove (June 25), Lee's attack on the Union right at Mechanicsville (June 26) was repulsed with great losses, but Lee and Jackson combined to defeat General Fitz-John Porter's V Corps in a bloody encounter at Gaines's Mill (June 27). In the battles of Peach Orchard and Savage's Station (June 29) and Frayser's Farm (Glendale; June 30), the retreating Union forces inflicted heavy casualties on the pursuing Confederates. Reaching the James River and supported by Union gunboats, the Northern troops turned back Lee's final assaults at Malvern Hill (July 1). Lee later stated in his official report

Document: Patriotic Songs of the North and South (1861)

Every war manifests its spirit in songs. One of the most popular songs of the North was "The Battle-Cry of Freedom," composed by George Frederick Root, a professional songwriter. The song was written a few hours after President Lincoln called for troops to put down the insurrection in Virginia. "The Bonnie Blue Flag" was one of the most popular Confederate songs, commemorating an early Confederate flag of solid blue with a white star. It was written by "the little Irishman," Harry McCarty, who grew famous singing it all over the South. According to one compiler of Confederate war songs, the people "went wild with excitement" when they heard the first familiar strains.

The Battle-Cry of Freedom

Yes, we'll rally round the flag, boys, we'll rally once again,
Shouting the battle-cry of freedom,
We will rally from the hillside, we'll gather from the plain,
Shouting the battle-cry of freedom.

Chorus:
The Union forever, hurrah! boys, hurrah!
Down with the traitor, up with the star,
While we rally round the flag, boys, rally once again,
Shouting the battle-cry of freedom....

The Bonnie Blue Flag

We are a band of brothers
And native to the soil,
Fighting for the property
We gained by honest toil;
And when our rights were threatened,
The cry rose near and far—
"Hurrah for the Bonnie Blue Flag
That bears the single star!"

Chorus:
Hurrah! hurrah!
For Southern rights, hurrah!
Hurrah for the Bonnie Blue Flag
That bears the single star....

Union field hospital, Savage's Station, Va. photograph by James F. Gibson, June 30, 1862. Library of Congress, Washington, D.C. (LC-B8171-0491 DLC)

that "Under ordinary circumstances the Federal Army should have been destroyed." McClellan's failure to capture Richmond, and the subsequent withdrawal of the Union's Army of the Potomac from the Yorktown Peninsula, signified the end of the Peninsular Campaign.

At the Second Battle of Bull Run (August 29–30), Lee drove another Union army, under Pope, out of Virginia and followed up by invading Maryland. McClellan was able to check Lee's forces at Antietam (or Sharpsburg, September 17).

Lee withdrew, regrouped, and dealt McClellan's successor, A.E. Burnside, a heavy defeat at Fredericksburg, Va., on December 13.

Burnside was in turn replaced as commander of the Army of the Potomac by Gen. Joseph Hooker. Following the "horror of Fredericksburg," Lee's Confederate army and Hooker's Union force had spent the winter facing each other across the Rappahannock River in Virginia. On April 27 Hooker dispatched his cavalry behind Lee's army, intending to cut off a retreat. Two days later he

Confederate soldiers dead by a fence on the Hagerstown road, Antietam, Md., photo by Alexander Gardner, September 1862. The Battle of Antietam was one of the most costly of the Civil War. Library of Congress, Washington, D.C. (LC-B8171-0560 DLC)

sent a small diversionary force across the Rappahannock below Fredericksburg and crossed upriver with the main body of his army. By May 1 his superior forces were massed near Chancellorsville, a crossroads in a densely forested lowland called the Wilderness. Deprived of his cavalry, however, Hooker was blind to Lee's movements, and on May 2, when Lee ordered Jackson's "foot cavalry" to swing around and attack the Union right, Hooker's

surprised flank was routed. The Union general withdrew, and Lee's pressure over the next three days forced a Union retreat north of the river. The South's greatest casualty was the loss of Jackson, who died May 10 of battle wounds.

Lee then undertook a second invasion of the North. He entered Pennsylvania, and a chance encounter of small units developed into a climactic battle at Gettysburg (July 1–3).

Battle of Gettysburg

Lee had decided to invade the North in hopes of further discouraging the enemy and possibly induc-ing European countries to recognize the Confederacy. His invasion army numbered 75,000 troops. Having learned that the Army of the Potomac had a new commander, Gen. George M. Meade, Lee ordered Gen. R.S. Ewell to move to Cashtown or Gettysburg, near Harrisburg, Pa. However, the com-mander of Meade's advance cavalry, Gen. John Buford, recognized the strategic importance of Gettysburg as a road centre and was prepared to hold this site until reinforcements arrived.

The first day of battle saw considerable fighting in the area, Union use of newly issued Spencer repeating carbines, heavy casualties on each side, and the simultaneous conclusion by both com-manders that Gettysburg was the place to fight. On the second day there were a great number of desperate attacks and counterattacks in an attempt to gain control of such locations as Little Round Top, Cemetery Hill, Devil's Den, the Wheatfield, and the Peach Orchard. There were again heavy losses on both sides.

On the third day Lee was determined to attack. Some 15,000 Confederate troops assaulted Cemetery Ridge, held by about 10,000 federal infantrymen. The Southern spearhead broke through and penetrated the ridge, but there it could do no more. Critically weakened by artillery during their approach, formations hopelessly tangled, lacking reinforcement, and under savage attack from three sides, the Southerners retreated, leaving 19 battle flags and hundreds of prisoners. On July 4 Lee waited to meet an attack that never came. That night, taking advantage of a heavy rain, he started retreating toward Virginia. His defeat stemmed from overconfidence in his troops, Ewell's inability to fill the boots of "Stonewall" Jackson, and faulty reconnaissance. Though Meade has

The battlefield of Gettysburg, photograph by Timothy O'Sullivan, July 1863. Library of Congress, Washington, D.C. (LC-B8184-7964-A DLC)

been criticized for not destroying the enemy by a vigorous pursuit, he had stopped the Confederate invasion and won a critical three-day battle.

Losses were among the war's heaviest: of 88,000 Northern troops, casualties numbered about 23,000 (with more than 3,100 killed); of 75,000 Southerners, there were between 20,000 and 28,000 casualties (with more than 4,500 killed).

At nearly the same time as the Confederate defeat at Gettysburg, a turning point was reached in the West. After two months of masterly maneuvering, Grant captured Vicksburg, Miss., on July 4, 1863. Soon the Mississippi River was entirely under Union control, effectively cutting the Confederacy in two. In October, after a Union army under Gen. W.S. Rosecrans had been defeated

Union soldiers wrecking railroad lines (making "Sherman's neckties"), Atlanta, Ga. Library of Congress, Washington, D.C. (B8184-10488)

at Chickamauga Creek, Ga. (September 19–20), Grant was called to take command in that theatre. Ably assisted by Gen. William Tecumseh Sherman and Gen. George Thomas, Grant drove Confederate general Braxton Bragg out of Chattanooga (November 23–25) and out of Tennessee; Sherman subsequently secured Knoxville.

In March 1864 Lincoln gave Grant supreme command of the Union armies. Grant took personal command of the

Document: Abraham Lincoln: The Gettysburg Address

After the Union victory at Gettysburg, a national commission was established to create the National Soldiers' Cemetery at Gettysburg for the several thousand soldiers, of both sides, who gave their lives in the battle. The dedication ceremony was planned for November 19. Edward Everett, former senator, former governor of Massachusetts, former president of Harvard, and a leading orator of the day, was chosen to give the major address. On November 2 President Lincoln was sent an invitation to attend and was requested to make "a few appropriate remarks" after Everett's speech. Lincoln accepted, though many other matters weighed on his mind. He was in the midst of preparing his annual message to Congress, and the events of the war required his constant attention. Having prepared a first draft of the speech he would make, Lincoln left Washington for Gettysburg on November 18 at a time when his son Tad lay sick in bed. During the late afternoon train ride the president seemed exceptionally weary. That night in his room Lincoln wrote the final draft of his speech, showing it only to Secretary of State Seward. Some 15,000 people were on Cemetery Hill for the ceremony when the president arrived. Everett spoke for nearly two hours; then the Baltimore Glee Club sang an ode; finally Ward Hill Lamon, Lincoln's military attaché, presented the president. Lincoln delivered the Gettysburg Address in three minutes and afterward leaned over to Lamon and said: "Lamon, that speech won't scour. It is a flat failure [and] the people won't like it." The following day Everett wrote Lincoln: "I should be glad if I could flatter myself that I came as near to the central idea of the occasion in two hours as you did in two minutes." Lincoln replied: "In our respective parts yesterday, you could not have been excused to make a short address, nor I a long one. I am pleased to know that, in your judgment, the little I did say was not entirely a failure."

Complete Works of Abraham Lincoln, *John G. Nicolay and John Hay, eds., New York, 1905, Vol. IX, pp. 209–210.*

Four score and seven years ago our fathers brought forth on this continent a new nation, conceived in liberty and dedicated to the proposition that all men are created equal.

Now we are engaged in a great civil war, testing whether that nation or any nation so conceived and so dedicated can long endure. We are met on a great battlefield of that war. We have come to dedicate a portion of that field as a final resting place for those who here gave their lives that that nation might live. It is altogether fitting and proper that we should do this.

But, in a larger sense, we cannot dedicate—we cannot consecrate—we cannot hallow—this ground. The brave men, living and dead, who struggled here have consecrated it far above our poor power to add or detract. The world will little note nor long remember what we say here, but it can never forget what they did here. It is for us, the living, rather, to be dedicated here to the unfinished work which they who fought here have thus far so nobly advanced.

It is rather for us to be here dedicated to the great task remaining before us—that from these honored dead we take increased devotion to that cause for which they gave the last full measure of devotion; that we here highly resolve that these dead shall not have died in vain; that this nation, under God, shall have a new birth of freedom; and that government of the people, by the people, for the people shall not perish from the earth.

Army of the Potomac in the east and soon formulated a strategy of attrition based upon the Union's overwhelming superiority in numbers and supplies. He began to move in May, suffering extremely heavy casualties in the battles of the Wilderness, Spotsylvania, and Cold Harbor, all in Virginia, and by mid-June he had Lee pinned down in fortifications before Petersburg, Va. For nearly 10 months the siege of Petersburg continued, while Grant slowly closed around Lee's positions. Meanwhile, Sherman faced the only other Confederate force of consequence in Georgia. Sherman captured Atlanta early in September, and in November he set out on his 300-mile (480-km) march through Georgia, leaving a swath of devastation behind him. He reached Savannah on December 10 and soon captured that city.

Document: Abraham Lincoln: Second Inaugural Address (1865)

As Lincoln prepared for his second inauguration in March 1865, there could be little doubt that the Confederacy would soon collapse. Lee's army was besieged at Petersburg, Union forces were pushing on to Richmond, and General Sherman had devastated Georgia and South Carolina. In the four years since he had assumed the presidency, Lincoln had greatly broadened his war aims. No longer were victory and political reunification his only objectives. He now set his sights on the greater task of the moral reconstruction of the nation. A year before he had expressed his vision in a letter to a Southern critic of his policy: "Now, at the end of three years' struggle, the nation's condition is not what either party, or any man devised, or expected. God alone can claim it.... If God now wills the removal of a great wrong [slavery], and wills also that we of the North as well as you of the South, shall pay fairly for our complicity in that wrong, impartial history will find therein new cause to attest and revere the justice and goodness of God." On March 4 Lincoln delivered his second inaugural address, with the realization that victory for the Union would pose even greater problems for the nation than the political schism preceding it. When Thurlow Weed, the New York journalist, complimented Lincoln on his rather brief speech, the president replied: "I expect the latter [Second Inaugural] to wear as well as—perhaps better than—anything I have produced; but I believe it is not immediately popular. Men are not flattered by being shown that there has been a difference of purpose between the Almighty and them.... It is truth which I thought needed to be told." Charles Francis Adams, Jr., recognized the significance of Lincoln's address better than most. "What do you think of the inaugural?" he asked. "That rail-splitting lawyer is one of the wonders of the day.... This inaugural strikes me... as being for all time the historical keynote of this war.... Not a prince or minister in all Europe could have risen to such an equality with the occasion." The speech was especially portentous for Lincoln in that John Wilkes Booth, who would assassinate him in the following month, was in the audience.

At this second appearing to take the oath of the presidential office, there is less occasion for an extended address than there was at the first. Then, a statement, somewhat in detail, of a course to be pursued seemed fitting and proper. Now, at the expiration of four years, during which public declarations have been constantly called forth on every point and phase of the great contest which still absorbs the attention and engrosses the energies of the nation, little that is new could be presented. The progress of our arms, upon which all else chiefly depends, is as well known to the public as to myself, and it is, I trust, reasonably satisfactory and encouraging to all. With high hope for the future, no prediction in regard to it is ventured.

On the occasion corresponding to this four years ago, all thoughts were anxiously directed to an impending civil war. All dreaded it, all sought to avert it. While the inaugural address was being delivered from this place, devoted altogether to saving the Union without war, insurgent agents were in the city seeking to destroy it without war—seeking to dissolve the Union and divide effects by negotiation. Both parties deprecated war, but one of them would make war rather than let the nation survive, and the other would accept war rather than let it perish. And the war came....

APPOMATTOX

By March 1865 Lee's army was thinned by casualties and desertions and was desperately short of supplies. Grant began his final advance on April 1 at Five Forks, captured Richmond on April 3, and accepted Lee's surrender at nearby Appomattox Court House on April 9. Sherman had moved north into North Carolina, and on April 26 he received the surrender of J.E. Johnston. The war was over.

Naval operations in the Civil War were secondary to the war on land, but there were nonetheless some celebrated exploits. David Farragut was justly hailed for his actions at New Orleans and at Mobile Bay (Aug. 5, 1864), and the battle

Document: George E. Pickett: The Night Before Appomattox (1865)

In the spring offensive of 1865, the Union armies repeatedly forced the Confederate armies to retreat and regroup. On March 31 and April 1, the division of Confederate Gen. George Pickett suffered heavy losses at Five Forks, west of Petersburg. Pickett took the fight to the enemy on the first day but was turned back; the counterattack on April 1 caught Pickett unprepared and the battle ended in a rout by the Union forces led by Gen. Philip Sheridan. Pickett himself narrowly escaped capture and, with the remainder of his command, joined Lee's forces near Appomattox. In the following letter to his wife, Pickett recorded his own and the Confederate Army's desperate situation. The letter is dated "Appomattox—Midnight—the night of the 8th and the dawn of the 9th," just prior to Lee's surrender.

I would have your life, my darling, all sunshine, all brightness. I would have no sorrow, no pain, no fear come to you but all

To be as cloudless, save with rare and roseate shadows

As I would thy fate.

The very thoughts of me that come to you must bring all that I would spare you.

Tomorrow may see our flag furled, forever.

Jackerie, our faithful old mail carrier, sobs behind me as I write. He bears tonight this—his last—message from me to you. He is commissioned with three orders, which I know you will obey as fearlessly as the bravest of your brother soldiers. Keep up a stout heart. Believe that I shall come back to you. Know that God reigns. After tonight, you will be my whole command—staff, field officers, men—all.

Lee's surrender is imminent. It is finished. Through the suggestion of their commanding officers as many of the men as desire are permitted to cut through and join Johnston's army. The cloud of despair settled over all on the 3rd, when the tidings came to us of the evacuation of Richmond and its partial loss by fire. The homes and families of many of my men were there, and all knew too well that with the fall of our capital, the last hope of success was over. And yet, my beloved, these men as resolutely obeyed the orders of their commanding officers as if we had just captured and burned the Federal capitol....

of the ironclads *Monitor* and *Virginia* (the rechristened *Merrimack*) on March 9, 1862, is often held to have opened the modern era of naval warfare. For the most part, however, the naval war was one of blockade as the Union attempted, largely successfully, to stop the Confederacy's commerce with Europe.

FOREIGN AFFAIRS

Davis and many Confederates expected recognition of their independence and direct intervention in the war on their behalf by Great Britain and possibly France. But they were cruelly disappointed, in part through the skillful

Confederate Gen. Robert E. Lee (right) *surrendering to Union Gen. Ulysses S. Grant at Appomattox Court House, Va., April 9, 1865; Currier & Ives hand-coloured lithograph.* Library of Congress Prints and Photographs Division

diplomacy of Lincoln, Secretary of State Seward, and the Union ambassador to England, Charles Francis Adams, and in part through Confederate military failure at a crucial stage of the war.

The Union's first trouble with Britain requiring some deft ex post facto diplomacy came when Captain Charles Wilkes halted the British steamer *Trent* on Nov. 8, 1861, and forcibly removed two Confederate envoys, James M. Mason and John Slidell, bound for Europe. Only the eventual release of the two men prevented a diplomatic rupture with Lord Palmerston's government in London. Another crisis erupted between the Union and England when the *Alabama*, built in the British Isles, was permitted upon completion to sail and join the Confederate navy, despite Adams's protestations. And when in September 1863 word reached the Lincoln government that two powerful rams—ironclad warships fitted with

Document: Walt Whitman: "Come Up from the Fields Father" (1865)

The Civil War had a great impact on Walt Whitman's life. He moved to Washington in 1863 and, after volunteering as a wound dresser in Washington hospitals, determined to devote his life to war service. His experiences during the war inspired many poems, a collection of which, Drum-Taps, *was published in 1865. "Come Up from the Fields Father," which appears to be based on a real incident, is one of his few attempts at characterization and dramatic presentation of a scene.* The New York Times, *in reviewing* Drum-Taps, *commented: "Mr. Whitman has fortunately better claims on the gratitude of his countrymen than any he will ever derive from his vocation as a poet.... His devotion to the most painful duties in the hospitals...will confer honor on his memory when...Drum-Taps have ceased to vibrate."*

Come up from the fields father, here's a letter from our Pete,
And come to the front door mother, here's a letter from thy dear son.
Lo, 'tis autumn,
Lo, where the trees, deeper green, yellower and redder,
Cool and sweeten Ohio's villages with leaves fluttering in the moderate wind,
Where apples ripe in the orchards hang and grapes on the trellised vines,
(Smell you the smell of the grapes on the vines?
Smell you the buckwheat where the bees were lately buzzing?)
Above all, lo, the sky so calm, so transparent after the rain, and with wondrous clouds,
Below too, all calm, all vital and beautiful, and the farm prospers well.
Down in the fields all prospers well,
But now from the fields come father, come at the daughter's call,
And come to the entry mother, to the front door come right away...

Document: Frank Wilkeson: How Americans Die in Battle (1864)

While there is no lack of written accounts about the Civil War, few ordinary soldiers in the war wrote extensively of their own personal experiences for public consumption. Frank Wilkeson was an exception. As a private and later an officer in the Union army, he wrote a brutally honest account of his war experiences, which he later published in Recollections of a Private Soldier in the Army of the Potomac. The excerpt reprinted here deals with events of the war in May 1864.

Almost every death on the battlefield is different. And the manner of the death depends on the wound and on the man, whether he is cowardly or brave, whether his vitality is large or small, whether he is a man of active imagination or is dull of intellect, whether he is of nervous or lymphatic temperament. I instance deaths and wounds that I saw in Grant's last campaign.

On the second day of the Battle of the Wilderness, where I fought as an infantry soldier, I saw more men killed and wounded than I did before or after in the same time. I knew but few of the men in the regiment in whose ranks I stood; but I learned the Christian names of some of them.

The man who stood next to me on my right was called Will. He was cool, brave, and intelligent. In the morning, when Corps II was advancing and driving Hill's soldiers slowly back, I was flurried. He noticed it and steadied my nerves by saying, kindly: "Don't fire so fast. This fight will last all day. Don't hurry. Cover your man before you pull the trigger. Take it easy, my boy, take it easy, and your cartridges will last the longer." This man fought effectively. During the day I had learned to look up to this excellent soldier and lean on him....

heavy metal beaks at the prows for piercing enemy ships—were being constructed in Britain for the Confederacy, Adams reputedly sent his famously succinct note to Britain's then-Foreign Secretary Lord John Russell stating, "It would be superfluous in me to point out to your lordship that this is war." In response the rams were seized by the British government at the last moment.

The diplomatic crisis of the Civil War came after Lee's striking victory at the Second Battle of Bull Run in late August 1862 and subsequent invasion of Maryland. The British government was set to offer mediation of the war and, if this was refused by the Lincoln administration (as it would have been), forceful intervention on behalf of the Confederacy. Only a victory by Lee on Northern soil was needed, but he was stopped by McClellan in September at Antietam, the Union's most needed success. The Confederate defeats at Gettysburg and Vicksburg the following summer ensured the continuing neutrality of Britain and

France, especially when Russia seemed inclined to favour the Northern cause. Even the growing British shortage of cotton from the Southern states did not force Palmerston's government into Davis's camp, particularly when British consuls in the Confederacy were more closely restricted toward the close of the war. In the final act, even the Confederate offer to abolish slavery in early 1865 in return for British recognition fell on deaf ears.

AFTERMATH

The war was horribly costly for both sides. The federal forces sustained more than a half million casualties (including nearly 360,000 deaths); the Confederate armies suffered about 483,000 casualties (approximately 258,000 deaths). Both governments, after strenuous attempts to finance loans, were obliged to resort to the printing press to make fiat money. While separate Confederate figures are lacking, the war finally cost the United States more than $15 billion. The South, especially, where most of the war was fought and which lost its labour system, was physically and economically devastated. In sum, although the Union was preserved and restored, the cost in physical and moral suffering was incalculable, and some spiritual wounds caused by the war still have not been healed.

CHAPTER 4

RECONSTRUCTION

Long portrayed by many historians as a time when vindictive Radical Republicans fastened black supremacy upon the defeated Confederacy, Reconstruction has since the late 20th century been viewed more sympathetically as a laudable experiment in interracial democracy. Reconstruction witnessed far-reaching changes in America's political life. At the national level, new laws and constitutional amendments permanently altered the federal system and the definition of American citizenship. In the South, a politically mobilized black community joined with white allies to bring the Republican Party to power, and with it a redefinition of the responsibilities of government.

RECONSTRUCTION UNDER ABRAHAM LINCOLN

The original Northern objective in the Civil War was the preservation of the Union—a war aim with which virtually everybody in the free states agreed. As the fighting progressed, the Lincoln government concluded that emancipation of the slaves was necessary in order to secure military victory; and thereafter freedom became a second war aim for the members of the Republican Party. The more radical members of that party—men such as Sen. Charles Sumner of Massachusetts and Rep. Thaddeus Stevens of Pennsylvania—believed that emancipation would prove a sham unless the government guaranteed the civil and political rights of the freedmen; thus, equality of all citizens before the law became a third war aim for this powerful faction. The fierce controversies of the Reconstruction era raged over which of these objectives should be insisted upon and how these goals should be secured.

LINCOLN'S PLAN

Lincoln himself had a flexible and pragmatic approach to Reconstruction, insisting only that the Southerners, when defeated, pledge future loyalty to the Union and emancipate their slaves. As the Southern states were subdued, he appointed military governors to supervise their restoration. The most vigorous and effective of these appointees was Andrew Johnson, a War Democrat whose success in reconstituting a loyal government in Tennessee led to his nomination as vice president on the Republican ticket with Lincoln in 1864. In December 1863

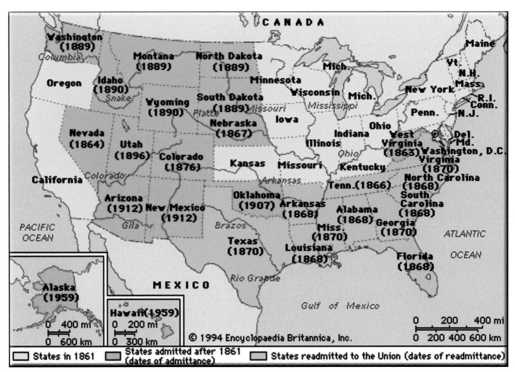

The United States after the Civil War, with dates of admittance of new states and dates readmitThe United States after the Civil War, showing admittance dates of new states and readmittance dates of the states of the former Confederacy.

Lincoln announced a general plan for the orderly Reconstruction of the Southern states, promising to recognize the government of any state that pledged to support the Constitution and the Union and to emancipate the slaves if it was backed by at least 10 percent of the number of voters in the 1860 presidential election. In Louisiana, Arkansas, and Tennessee loyal governments were formed under Lincoln's plan; and they sought readmission to the Union with the seating of their senators and representatives in Congress.

THE RADICALS' PLAN

Radical Republicans were outraged at these procedures, which reflected executive usurpation of congressional powers, which required only minimal changes in the Southern social system, and which left political power essentially in the hands of the same Southerners who had led their states out of the Union. The Radicals put forth their own plan of Reconstruction in the Wade–Davis Bill, which Congress passed on July 2, 1864; it required not 10 percent but a majority of the white male citizens in each Southern state to participate in the reconstruction process, and it insisted upon an oath of past, not just of future, loyalty. Finding the bill too rigorous and inflexible, Lincoln pocket vetoed it; and the Radicals bitterly denounced him. During the 1864–65 session of Congress, they in turn defeated the president's proposal to recognize the Louisiana government organized under his 10 percent plan. At the time of Lincoln's assassination by John Wilkes Booth on April 14, 1865, therefore, the president and the Congress were at loggerheads over Reconstruction.

The Assassination of Abraham Lincoln

On the morning of April 14, 1865, actor and Confederate sympathizer John Wilkes Booth—distraught over the collapse of the Confederacy—learned that Pres. Abraham Lincoln would be attending a performance of the comedy **Our American Cousin** *that evening at Ford's Theatre in Washington, D.C. Booth was a member of one of America's most renowned families of actors. He grew up in the border state of Maryland but was particularly popular as an actor in Richmond, Va., and considered himself a Southerner. Having promised his mother that he would not fight for the Confederacy, Booth remained in the North during the Civil War, where his hatred of abolitionists and Lincoln deepened. In March 1865 he and a group of conspirators in Washington, D.C., had plotted to abduct Lincoln; however, none of those plans came to fruition.*

After learning of Lincoln's theatre plans, Booth again gathered his fellow conspirators and outlined a plan to assassinate not just the president but also Vice Pres. Andrew Johnson and Secretary of State William Seward. Booth tasked Lewis Powell, a former Confederate soldier, with the attack on Seward, to be aided by David Herold. George Atzerodt, a German immigrant who had acted as a boatman for Confederate spies, was to kill Johnson. Booth himself was to assassinate Lincoln. All three attacks were to occur at the same time (about 10:00 PM) that night.

In the event, Atzerodt failed to carry out his assignment and never approached Johnson. Powell invaded Seward's home and slashed him repeatedly with a knife. Seward survived the attack, but his face was permanently disfigured.

At Ford's Theatre Booth made his way to the private box in which Lincoln and his wife, Mary Todd Lincoln, were watching the play with their guests, Clara Harris and her fiancé, Union officer Maj. Henry Rathbone. Finding the president's box essentially unguarded, Booth entered it and barred the outside door from inside. Then, at a moment in the play that he knew would elicit a big laugh, Booth burst in through the box's inner door. He shot Lincoln in the back of the head once with a derringer, slashed Rathbone in the shoulder with a knife, and leapt from the box to the stage below, breaking his left leg in the fall (though some believe that injury did not occur until later). What Booth said while committing the attack and when he said it are a matter of some dispute. Audience members variously reported that he exclaimed, "Sic semper tyrannis!" ("Thus always to tyrants," the state motto of Virginia) or "The South is avenged!" or both, before disappearing through a door at the side of the stage where his horse was being held for him. In any case, Booth rode off into the night and out of Washington, meeting up in Maryland with Herold, who had fled the scene of the Seward attack without Powell.

Lincoln was attended to immediately by several doctors who were in the audience. It was felt that the president should not be moved far, so he was taken across the street to the house of William Petersen, who rented extra rooms to lodgers. In one of those rooms Lincoln was laid diagonally across a bed, for which he was otherwise too tall. Doctors had little hope that the unconscious Lincoln would recover, and throughout the night various cabinet members, officials, and physicians kept vigil in the small room. Mary grieved hysterically. When Lincoln was pronounced dead at 7:22 AM on April 15, Secretary of War Edwin M. Stanton famously pronounced, "Now he belongs to the ages" (or "to the angels"; witnesses disagree).

A period of national mourning ensued. Observers reported that African Americans felt Lincoln's loss particularly keenly. After public viewing in both the White House and the Capitol, Lincoln's body, in an elaborate open coffin, was taken on a circuitous 13-day train journey back to his home in Springfield, Ill., stopping en route to lie in state in Independence Hall in Philadelphia and to be paraded in a hearse down 5th Avenue in New York City, among other stops. Millions of people lined the train route to pay their respects.

While a massive manhunt, fueled by a $100,000 reward, filled the countryside surrounding Washington with troops and other searchers, Booth and Herold, aided by a Confederate sympathizer, hid for days in a thicket of trees near the Zekiah swamp in Maryland. Having undertaken further efforts to escape, Booth and Herold were tracked down by federal troops on April 26 at a farm in Virginia, near the Rappahannock River. There Herold surrendered before the barn in which he and Booth were hiding was set aflame. Refusing to surrender, Booth was shot, either by a soldier or by himself, and died shortly thereafter.

Eight "conspirators" were tried by a military commission for Lincoln's murder (several of them had participated in the plot to kidnap Lincoln but were less clearly involved in the assassination attempt). Four were found guilty and hanged; four others were imprisoned.

RECONSTRUCTION UNDER ANDREW JOHNSON

Following the assassination, Johnson became president and inaugurated the period of Presidential Reconstruction. At first it seemed that Johnson might be able to work more cooperatively with Congress in the process of Reconstruction. A former representative and a former senator, he understood congressmen. A loyal Unionist who had stood by his country even at the risk of his life when Tennessee seceded, he was certain not to compromise with secession; and his experience as military governor of that state showed him to be politically shrewd and tough toward the slaveholders. "Johnson, we have faith in you," Radical Benjamin F. Wade assured the new president on the day he took the oath of office. "By the gods, there will be no trouble running the government."

PRESIDENTIAL RECONSTRUCTION

Such Radical trust in Johnson proved misplaced. The new president was, first

Andrew Johnson, photographed by Mathew Brady. Library of Congress, Washington, D.C.

of all, himself a Southerner. He was a Democrat who looked for the restoration of his old party partly as a step toward his own reelection to the presidency in 1868. Johnson offered a pardon to all Southern whites except Confederate leaders and wealthy planters (although most of these subsequently received individual pardons), restoring their political rights and all property except slaves. He also outlined how new state governments would be created. Apart from the requirement that they abolish slavery, repudiate secession, and abrogate the Confederate debt, these governments were granted a free hand in managing their affairs. They responded by enacting the Black Cdes, laws that required African Americans to sign yearly labour contracts and in other ways sought to limit the freedmen's economic options and reestablish plantation discipline. African Americans strongly resisted the implementation of these measures, and they seriously undermined Northern support for Johnson's policies.

When Congress assembled in December 1865, Radical Republicans such as Stevens and. Sumner called for the establishment of new Southern governments based on equality before the law and universal male suffrage. But the more numerous moderate Republicans

Document: Civil Rights Act (1866)

The Civil Rights Act of April 9, 1866, conferred citizenship on African Americans and was designed to supersede the 1857 Dred Scott *decision and such discriminatory legislation as the Mississippi Black Codes. It was the first federal statute to define citizenship and to guarantee civil rights within states. Because there was some doubt in Congress as to the constitutionality of the act, its more prominent features were later incorporated in the Fourteenth Amendment. Pres. Andrew Johnson had vetoed the act in March 1866, but his opponents in Congress gathered enough votes to pass the bill over his veto. The ability to override presidential vetoes made it clear that Congress was assuming full control of the Reconstruction program. Portions of the act follow.*

Be it enacted by the Senate and House of Representatives of the United States of America in Congress assembled, that all persons born in the United States and not subject to any foreign power, excluding Indians not taxed, are hereby declared to be citizens of the United States; and such citizens, of every race and color, without regard to any previous condition of slavery or involuntary servitude, except as a punishment for crime whereof the party shall have been duly convicted, shall have the same right, in every state and territory in the United States, to make and enforce contracts; to sue; be parties, and give evidence; to inherit, purchase, lease, sell, hold, and convey real and personal property; and to full and equal benefit of all laws and proceedings for the security of person and property as is enjoyed by white citizens, and shall be subject to like punishment, pains, and penalties, and to none other, any law, statute, ordinance, regulation, or custom to the contrary notwithstanding....

hoped to work with Johnson while modifying his program. Congress refused to seat the representatives and senators elected from the Southern states and in early 1866 passed the Freedmen's Bureau Bill, which extended the life of an agency Congress had created in 1865 to oversee the transition from slavery to freedom, and the Civil Rights Bill.

A combination of personal stubbornness, fervent belief in states' rights, and racist convictions led Johnson to reject both the Freedmen's Bureau and the Civil Rights bills, causing a permanent rupture between himself and Congress. The Civil Rights Act became the first significant legislation in American history to become law over a president's veto. Shortly thereafter, Congress approved the Fourteenth Amendment, which put the principle of birthright citizenship

Thaddeus Stevens, photo by Mathew Brady. Library of Congress, Washington, D.C.

into the Constitution and forbade states to deprive any citizen of the "equal

Document: Andrew Johnson: Against the Radical Republicans (1866)

On the evening of Feb. 22, 1866, Pres. Andrew Johnson delivered an impromptu address to a crowd of citizens gathered on the White House lawn in celebration of George Washington's birthday. Johnson expressed annoyance at congressional criticism of his veto of the Freedmen's Bureau Bill three days before. As the president's advisers had warned, the speech was fully reported in the next day's newspapers and drew an outburst of angry public reaction.

I have already remarked that there were two parties—one for destroying the government to preserve slavery, and the other to break up the government to destroy slavery. The objects to be accomplished were different, it is true, so far as slavery is concerned, but they agreed in one thing, and that was the breaking up of the government. They agreed in the destruction of the government, the precise thing which I have already stood up to oppose. Whether the disunionists come from the South or the North, I stand now where I did then, to vindicate the Union of these states and the Constitution of the country....

Who, I ask, has suffered more for the Union than I have? I shall not now repeat the wrongs or suffering inflicted upon me; but it is not the way to deal with a whole people in the spirit of revenge.... There is no one who has labored harder than I have to have the principal conscious and intelligent traitors brought to justice; to have the law vindicated, and the great fact vindicated that treason is a crime. Yet, while conscious, intelligent traitors are to be punished, should whole states, communities, and people be made to submit to and bear the penalty of death? I have, perhaps, as much hostility and as much resentment as a man ought to have; but we should conform our action and our conduct to the example of Him who founded our holy religion....

protection" of the laws. Arguably the most important addition to the Constitution other than the Bill of Rights, the amendment constituted a profound change in federal-state relations. Traditionally, citizens' rights had been delineated and protected by the states. Thereafter, the federal government would guarantee all Americans' equality before the law against state violation.

Document: Fourteenth Amendment (1866)

The Fourteenth and Fifteenth Amendments were devised by the Republican members of Congress as part of their Reconstruction program. The Fourteenth, ratified in July 1868, conferred citizenship upon African Americans; ratification was a precondition of readmission to the Union for the Confederate states. The "due process" clause of this amendment came to have great significance in subsequent decades as the "persons" mentioned in Section 1 were understood by the courts to be business corporations as well as individuals.

Section 1. All persons born or naturalized in the United States and subject to the jurisdiction thereof are citizens of the United States and of the state wherein they reside. No state shall make or enforce any law which shall abridge the privileges or immunities of citizens of the United States; nor shall any state deprive any person of life, liberty, or property without due process of law; nor deny to any person within its jurisdiction the equal protection of the laws.

Section 2. Representatives shall be apportioned among the several states according to their respective numbers, counting the whole number of persons in each state, excluding Indians not taxed. But when the right to vote at any election for the choice of electors for President and Vice-President of the United States, representatives in Congress, the executive and judicial officers of a state, or the members of the legislature thereof, is denied to any of the male inhabitants of such state, being twenty-one years of age, and citizens of the United States, or in any way abridged, except for participation in rebellion or other crime, the basis of representation therein shall be reduced in the proportion which the number of such male citizens shall bear to the whole number of male citizens twenty-one years of age in such state....

RADICAL RECONSTRUCTION

In the fall 1866 congressional elections, Northern voters overwhelmingly repudiated Johnson's policies. Congress decided to begin Reconstruction anew. The Reconstruction Acts of 1867 divided the South into five military districts and

"This Is a White Man's Government," political cartoon by Thomas Nast, published in Harper's Weekly, *Sept. 5, 1868. Depicted standing atop a black Civil War veteran are a "Five Points Irishman," Ku Klux Klan founder Nathan Bedford Forrest, and Wall Street financier and Democrat August Belmont.* Thomas Nast/Library of Congress, Washington, D.C. (neg. no. LC-USZ62-121735)

outlined how new governments, based on manhood suffrage without regard to race, were to be established. Thus began the period of Radical or Congressional Reconstruction, which lasted until the end of the last Southern Republican governments in 1877.

SOUTHERN REPUBLICANS

By 1870 all the former Confederate states had been readmitted to the Union, and nearly all were controlled by the Republican Party. Three groups made up Southern Republicanism. Carpetbaggers, or recent arrivals from the North, were former Union soldiers, teachers, Freedmen's Bureau agents, and businessmen. The second large group, scalawags, or native-born white Republicans, included some businessmen and planters, but most were nonslaveholding small farmers from the Southern up-country. Loyal to the Union during the Civil War, they saw the Republican Party as a means of keeping Confederates from regaining power in the South.

The third group was African Americans, who formed the overwhelming majority of Southern Republican voters in every state. From the

Document: Report of the Joint Committee on Reconstruction (1866)

The Joint Committee on Reconstruction was created by Congress in December 1865 to investigate and make recommendations on all bills relating to Reconstruction. The Committee consisted of nine representatives and six senators; only three members were Democrats, the dominant Republican bloc being led by Rep. Thaddeus Stevens. The Committee's Report of June 20, 1866, on the status of the South reflected the Radical views of the majority of the members. An extract from the introduction to the report is reprinted here.

When Congress assembled in December last, the people of most of the states lately in rebellion had, under the advice of the President, organized local governments, and some of them had acceded to the terms proposed by him. In his annual message he stated, in general terms, what had been done, but he did not see fit to communicate the details for the information of Congress. While in this and in a subsequent message the President urged the speedy restoration of these states, and expressed the opinion that their condition was such as to justify their restoration, yet it is quite obvious that Congress must either have acted blindly on that opinion of the President, or proceeded to obtain the information requisite for intelligent action on the subject. The impropriety of proceeding wholly on the judgment of any one man, however exalted his station, in a matter involving the welfare of the republic in all future time, or of adopting any plan, coming from any source, without fully understanding all its bearings and comprehending its full effect, was apparent....

beginning of Reconstruction, black conventions and newspapers throughout the South had called for the extension of full civil and political rights to African Americans. Composed of those who had been free before the Civil War plus slave ministers, artisans, and Civil War veterans, the black political leadership pressed for the elimination of the racial caste system and the economic uplifting of the former slaves. Sixteen African Americans served in Congress during Reconstruction—including Hiram Revels and Blanche K. Bruce in the U.S. Senate—more than 600 in state legislatures, and hundreds more in local offices from sheriff to justice of the peace scattered across the South. So-called "black supremacy" never existed, but the advent of African Americans in

Hiram Revels (seated at far left) *of Mississippi, the first African American U.S. senator, along with black members of the House of Representatives* (seated, left to right) *Benjamin S. Turner of Alabama, Josiah T. Walls of Florida, and Joseph H. Rainey and Robert Brown Elliott of South Carolina and* (standing) *Robert C. Delarge of South Carolina and Jefferson H. Long of Georgia.* Library of Congress, Washington, D.C. (neg. no. LC-USZC2-2325)

positions of political power marked a dramatic break with the country's traditions and aroused bitter hostility from Reconstruction's opponents.

Serving an expanded citizenry, Reconstruction governments established the South's first state-funded public school systems, sought to strengthen the bargaining power of plantation labourers, made taxation more equitable, and outlawed racial discrimination in public transportation and

Blanche K. Bruce, senator from Mississippi. Library of Congress, Washington, D.C.

accommodations. They also offered lavish aid to railroads and other enterprises in the hope of creating a "New South" whose economic expansion would benefit blacks and whites alike. But the economic program spawned corruption and rising taxes, alienating increasing numbers of white voters.

FORTY ACRES AND A MULE

Meanwhile, the social and economic transformation of the South proceeded apace. To blacks, freedom meant independence from white control. Reconstruction provided the opportunity for African Americans to solidify their family ties and to create independent religious institutions, which became centres of community life that survived long after Reconstruction ended. The former slaves also demanded economic independence. Blacks' hopes that the federal government would provide them with land had been raised by Gen. William T. Sherman's Field Order No. 15 of January 1865, which set aside a large swath of land along the coast of South Carolina and Georgia for the exclusive settlement of black families, and by the Freedmen's Bureau Act of March, which authorized the bureau to rent or sell land in its possession to former slaves. But President Johnson in the summer of 1865 ordered land in federal hands to be returned to its former owners. The dream of "40 acres and a mule" was stillborn. Lacking land, most former slaves had little economic alternative other than resuming work on plantations owned by whites. Some worked for wages, others as sharecroppers, who divided the crop with the owner at the end of the year. Neither status offered much hope for economic mobility. For decades, most Southern blacks remained propertyless and poor.

Nonetheless, the political revolution of Reconstruction spawned increasingly violent opposition from white Southerners. White supremacist organizations that committed terrorist acts, such as the Ku Klux Klan, targeted local Republican leaders for beatings or assassination. African Americans who asserted their rights in dealings with white employers, teachers, ministers, and others seeking to assist the former slaves also became targets. At Colfax, La., in 1873, scores of black militiamen were killed after surrendering to armed whites intent on seizing control of local government. Increasingly, the new Southern governments looked to Washington, D.C., for assistance.

By 1869 the Republican Party was firmly in control of all three branches of the federal government. After attempting to remove Secretary of War Edwin M. Stanton, in violation of the new Tenure of Office Act, Johnson had been impeached by the House of Representatives in 1868. Although the Senate, by a single vote, failed to remove him from office, Johnson's power to obstruct the course of Reconstruction

Wood engraving, c. 1866, depicting two members of the Ku Klux Klan. Dressed in robes and sheets designed to frighten African Americans and prevent identification by the occupying federal troops, Klansmen whipped and killed freedmen and their white supporters in nighttime raids of terror and destruction. MPI/Archive Photos/Getty Images was gone. Republican Ulysses S. Grant was elected president that fall.

RECONSTRUCTION UNDER ULYSSES S. GRANT

During the two administrations of President Grant there was a gradual attrition of Republican strength. As a politician the president was passive, exhibiting none of the brilliance he had shown on the battlefield. His administration was tarnished by the dishonesty of his subordinates, whom he loyally defended. As the older Radical leaders—men such as Sumner, Wade, and Stevens—died, leadership in the Republican Party fell into the hands of technicians such as Roscoe Conkling and James G. Blaine, men devoid of the idealistic fervour that had marked the early Republicans. At the same time, many Northerners were growing tired of the whole Reconstruction issue and were weary of the annual outbreaks of violence in the South that required repeated use of federal force.

Efforts to shore up the Radical regimes in the South grew increasingly unsuccessful. The adoption of the Fifteenth Amendment (1870), prohibiting discrimination in voting on account of race, had little effect in the South, where terrorist organizations and economic pressure from planters kept African Americans from the polls. Nor were three Force Acts passed by the Republicans (1870–71), giving the president the power to suspend the writ of habeas corpus and imposing heavy penalties upon terroristic organizations, in the long run more successful. If they succeeded in dispersing the Ku Klux Klan as an organization, they also drove its members, and their tactics, more than ever into the Democratic camp.

Document: Federal Grand Jury Report on the Ku Klux Klan (1871)

The Ku Klux Klan, like the Knights of the White Camelia and other secret societies, attempted to restore white social and political supremacy despite the contrary provisions of the Fourteenth Amendment. The activities of the most active Klan group, in South Carolina, led President Grant to exercise his powers to enforce the Amendment. He suspended the right of habeas corpus in nine South Carolina counties in October 1871, and several military arrests followed. At the same time a grand jury was summoned in Columbia to investigate the activities of the Klan. A portion of the report of the grand jury follows, addressed to the judges of the U.S. Circuit Court.

During the whole session we have been engaged in investigations of the most grave and extraordinary character—investigations of the crimes committed by the organization known as the Ku Klux Klan. The evidence elicited has been voluminous, gathered from the victims themselves and their families, as well as those who belong to the Klan and participated in its crimes. The jury has been shocked beyond measure at the developments which have been made in their presence of the number and character of the atrocities committed, producing a state of terror and a sense of utter insecurity among a large portion of the people, especially the colored population. The evidence produced before us has established the following facts:

- *That there has existed since 1868, in many counties of the state, an organization known as the "Ku Klux Klan," or "Invisible Empire of the South," which embraces in its membership a large proportion of the white population of every profession and class.*
- *That this Klan [is] bound together by an oath, administered to its members at the time of their initiation into the order, of which the following is a copy:*

OBLIGATION

I [name], before the immaculate Judge of Heaven and earth, and upon the Holy Evangelists of Almighty God, do, of my own free will and accord, subscribe to the following sacredly binding obligation:

- *We are on the side of justice, humanity, and constitutional liberty, as bequeathed to us in its purity by our forefathers.*
- *We oppose and reject the principles of the Radical Party....*

SOUTHERN "HOME RULE"

Growing Northern disillusionment with Radical Reconstruction and with the Grant administration became evident in the Liberal Republican movement of 1872, which resulted in the nomination of the erratic Horace Greeley for president. Though Grant was overwhelmingly reelected, the true temper of the country was demonstrated in the congressional elections of 1874, which gave the Democrats control of the House of Representatives for the first time since the outbreak of the Civil War. Despite Grant's hope for a third term in office, most Republicans recognized by 1876 that it was time to change both the candidate and his Reconstruction program, and the nomination of Rutherford B. Hayes of Ohio, a moderate Republican of high principles and of deep sympathy for the South, marked the end of the Radical domination of the Republican Party.

The circumstances surrounding the disputed election of 1876 strengthened Hayes's intention to work with the Southern whites, even if it meant abandoning the few Radical regimes that remained in the South. In an election marked by widespread fraud and many irregularities, the Democratic candidate, Samuel J. Tilden, received the majority of the popular vote; but the vote in the electoral college was long in doubt. In order to resolve the impasse, Hayes's lieutenants had to enter into agreement with Southern Democratic congressmen, promising to withdraw the remaining federal troops from the South, to share the Southern patronage with Democrats, and to favour that section's demands for federal subsidies in the building of levees and railroads. Hayes's inauguration marked, for practical purposes, the restoration of "home rule" for the South—i.e., that the North would no longer interfere in Southern elections to protect African Americans and that the Southern whites would again take control of their state governments.

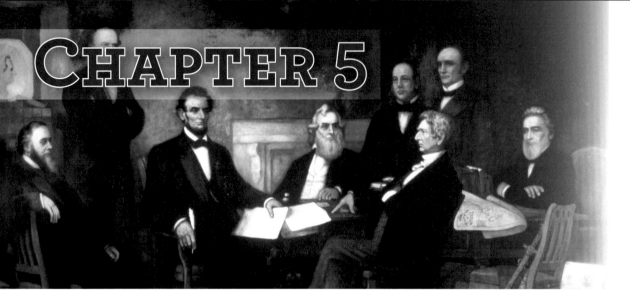

CHAPTER 5

THE NEW SOUTH

In the wake of the war and Reconstruction, some spoke of the emergence of a "New South," marked by profound changes to the region's political, economic, and social organization. The New South had no more forceful advocate than Henry Grady, the editor of the *Atlanta Constitution*, who argued that the post-plantation South had embraced modern entrepreneurial capitalism and industrialism. Grady also acknowledged the importance of accepting and empowering a changed role for African Americans in Southern society; however, his view of the New South proved to be different from that of many other white Southerners.

THE ERA OF CONSERVATIVE DOMINATION

The Republican regimes in the Southern states began to fall as early as 1870; by 1877 they had all collapsed. For the next 13 years the South was under the leadership of white Democrats whom their critics called Bourbons because, like the French royal family, they supposedly had learned nothing and forgotten nothing from the revolution they had experienced. For the South as a whole, the characterization is neither quite accurate nor quite fair. In most Southern states the new political leaders represented not only the planters but also the rising Southern business community, interested in railroads, cotton textiles, and urban land speculation.

Even on racial questions the new Southern political leaders were not so reactionary as the label Bourbon might suggest. Though whites were in the majority in all but two of the Southern states, the conservative regimes did not attempt to disfranchise African Americans. Partly their restraint was caused by fear of further federal intervention; chiefly, however, it stemmed from a conviction on the part of conservative leaders that they could control African American voters, whether through fraud, intimidation, or manipulation.

Indeed, African American votes were sometimes of great value to these regimes, which favoured the businessmen and planters of the South at the expense of the small white farmers. These "Redeemer" governments sharply reduced or even eliminated the programs of the state governments that benefited poor people. The public school system was starved for money; in 1890 the per capita expenditure in the South for public education was only 97 cents, as compared with $2.24 in the country as a whole. The care of state prisoners, the insane, and the blind was also neglected; and measures to safeguard the public health were rejected. At the same time these conservative regimes were often astonishingly corrupt, and

embezzlement and defalcation on the part of public officials were even greater than during the Reconstruction years.

The small white farmers resentful of planter dominance, residents of the hill country outvoted by Black Belt constituencies, and politicians excluded from the ruling cabals tried repeatedly to overthrow the conservative regimes in the South. During the 1870s they supported Independent or Greenback Labor candidates, but without notable success. In 1879 the Readjuster Party in Virginia— so named because its supporters sought to readjust the huge funded debt of that state so as to lessen the tax burden on small farmers—gained control of the legislature and secured in 1880 the election of its leader, Gen. William Mahone, to the U.S. Senate. Not until 1890, however, when the powerful Farmers' Alliance, hitherto devoted exclusively to the promotion of agricultural reforms, dropped its ban on politics, was there an effective challenge to conservative hegemony. In that year, with Alliance backing, Benjamin R. Tillman was chosen governor of South Carolina and James S. Hogg was elected governor of Texas; the heyday of Southern populism was at hand.

JIM CROW LEGISLATION

African American voting in the South was a casualty of the conflict between Redeemers and Populists. Although some Populist leaders, such as Tom Watson in Georgia, saw that poor whites and poor blacks in the South

Stretching from the end of Reconstruction to the beginning of a strong civil rights movement in the 1950s, Jim Crow laws of the South enforced racial segregation. This theatre in Leland, Miss., shown in 1939, was one such segregated facility. Marion Post Wolcott/Archive Photos/Getty Images

had a community of interest in the struggle against the planters and the businessmen, most small white farmers exhibited vindictive hatred toward African Americans, whose votes had so often been instrumental in upholding conservative regimes. Beginning in 1890, when Mississippi held a new constitutional convention, and continuing through 1908, when Georgia amended its constitution, every state of the former Confederacy moved to disfranchise African Americans. Because

the U.S. Constitution forbade outright racial discrimination, the Southern states excluded African Americans by requiring that potential voters be able to read or to interpret any section of the Constitution—a requirement that local registrars waived for whites but rigorously insisted upon when an audacious black wanted to vote. Louisiana, more ingenious, added the "grandfather clause" to its constitution, which exempted from this literacy test all of those who had been entitled to vote

Document: Frederick Douglass: The Colour Line in America (1883)

After 1877, following the withdrawal of Union troops from South Carolina, Louisiana, and Florida, Reconstruction officially ended. In theory, African Americans were free, but in practice, their status was far from equal. The intent of the Fourteenth and Fifteenth Amendments with regard to African Americans was being whittled away by state legislation in the South and Supreme Court decisions. African American participation in all phases of American life was qualified by prejudice; most avenues of social and economic improvement remained closed. Frederick Douglass, the best-known and most influential African American spokesman of his time, considered these facts and offered a solution in the following speech of Sept. 24, 1883.

It is our lot to live among a people whose laws, traditions, and prejudices have been against us for centuries, and from these they are not yet free. To assume that they are free from these evils simply because they have changed their laws is to assume what is utterly unreasonable and contrary to facts. Large bodies move slowly. Individuals may be converted on the instant and change their whole course of life. Nations never. Time and events are required for the conversion of nations. Not even the character of a great political organization can be changed by a new platform. It will be the same old snake though in a new skin.

Though we have had war, reconstruction, and abolition as a nation, we still linger in the shadow and blight of an extinct institution. Though the colored man is no longer subject to be bought and sold, he is still surrounded by an adverse sentiment which fetters all his movements. In his downward course he meets with no resistance, but his course upward is resented and resisted at every step of his progress. If he comes in ignorance, rags, and wretchedness, he conforms to the popular belief of his character, and in that character he is welcome. But if he shall come as a gentleman, a scholar, and a statesman, he is hailed as a contradiction to the national faith concerning his race, and his coming is resented as impudence. In the one case he may provoke contempt and derision, but in the other he is an affront to pride and provokes malice. Let him do what he will, there is at present, therefore, no escape for him. The color line meets him everywhere, and in a measure shuts him out from all respectable and profitable trades and callings....

on Jan. 1, 1867—i.e., before Congress imposed African American suffrage upon the South—together with their sons and grandsons. Other states imposed stringent property qualifications for voting or enacted complex poll taxes.

Socially as well as politically, race relations in the South deteriorated as farmers' movements rose to challenge the conservative regimes. By 1890, with the triumph of Southern populism, the African American's place was clearly

Document: Booker T. Washington: The Road to African American Progress (1895)

Booker T. Washington, first principal and chief developer of Tuskegee Institute in Alabama. Library of Congress, Washington, D.C.

In his introduction of speaker Booker T. Washington to the audience at the Cotton States and International Exposition in Atlanta, Ga., on Sept. 18, 1895, former Georgia governor Rufus Bullock called Washington a "representative of Negro enterprise and Negro civilization." In his speech, which thrust him onto the national stage, Washington allayed any fears his white audience might have had about the ambitions of Southern African Americans. Washington emphasized that African Americans wanted responsibilities rather than rights and proposed a program of accommodation that pleased white Southerners. The result was that Washington assumed the role of spokesperson for African Americans. Washington inherited this role from Frederick Douglass, who had died earlier in the year.

One-third of the population of the South is of the Negro race. No enterprise seeking the material, civil, or moral welfare of this section can disregard this element of our population and reach the highest success. I but convey to you, Mr. President and Directors, the sentiment of the masses of my race when I say that in no way have the value and manhood of the American Negro been more fittingly and generously recognized than by the managers of this magnificent exposition at every stage of its progress. It is a recognition that will do more to cement the friendship of the two races than any occurrence since the dawn of our freedom.

Not only this, but the opportunity here afforded will awaken among us a new era of industrial progress. Ignorant and inexperienced, it is not strange that in the first years of our new life we began at the top instead of at the bottom; that a seat in Congress or the state legislature was more sought than real estate or industrial skill; that the political convention or stump speaking had more attractions than starting a dairy farm or truck garden....

defined by law; he was relegated to a subordinate and entirely segregated position. Not only were legal sanctions (some reminiscent of the "Black Codes") being imposed upon African Americans, but informal, extralegal, and often brutal steps were also being taken to keep them in their "place." From 1889 to 1899, lynchings in the South averaged 187.5 per year.

BOOKER T. WASHINGTON AND THE ATLANTA COMPROMISE

Faced with implacable and growing hostility from Southern whites, many African Americans during the 1880s and '90s felt that their only sensible course was to avoid open conflict and to work out some pattern of accommodation. The most influential African American spokesman for this policy was Booker T. Washington, the head of Tuskegee Institute in Alabama, who urged his fellow African Americans to forget about politics and college education in the classical languages and to learn how to be better farmers and artisans. With thrift, industry, and abstention from politics, he thought that African Americans could gradually win the respect of their white neighbours. In 1895, in a speech at the opening of the Atlanta Cotton States and International Exposition, Washington most fully elaborated his position, which became known as the Atlanta Compromise.

Abjuring hopes of federal intervention on behalf of African Americans, Washington argued that reform in the South would have to come from within. Change could best be brought about if blacks and whites recognized that "the agitation of questions of social equality is the extremest folly"; in the social life the races in the South could be as separate as the fingers, but in economic progress as united as the hand.

Enthusiastically received by Southern whites, Washington's program also found many adherents among Southern blacks, who saw in his doctrine a way to avoid head-on, disastrous confrontations with overwhelming white force. Whether or not Washington's plan would have produced a generation of orderly, industrious, frugal African Americans slowly working themselves into middle-class status is not known because of the intervention of a profound economic depression throughout the South during most of the post-Reconstruction period. Neither poor whites nor poor blacks had much opportunity to rise in a region that was desperately impoverished. By 1890 the South ranked lowest in every index that compared the sections of the United States—lowest in per capita income, public health, and lowest in education. In short, by the 1890s the South, a poor and backward region, had yet to recover from the ravages of the Civil War or to reconcile itself to the readjustments required by the Reconstruction era.

Conclusion

Slavery and what to do, or not do, about it had been at the heart of discussions regarding the American future since the founding of the United States. A series of compromises that ultimately satisfied neither advocates of slavery nor its opponents—from the Constitution's codification of a slave as three-fifths of a person in determining legislative representation to the Compromise of 1850—merely forestalled the eventual resolution of the issue, which took a great civil war to decide. That conflict, often cited as the first modern "total" war, left its mark not only on the millions who fought in it and the hundreds of thousands who died as a result of it but also on generations that followed. Notwithstanding the wide spectrum of opinion in both the North and the South regarding slavery and the place of African Americans in American society, there is little doubt that the war ostensibly fought initially to preserve the Union had the South's "peculiar institution" at its roots and had emancipation as its most important outcome. The war and the period of Reconstruction brought the promise of change as well as real change for African Americans. However, in a remarkably short time a retrenchment of the old order followed in the guise of Jim Crow laws, poll taxes, "grandfather clauses," servitude-like sharecropping, and segregation. As a result, the struggle for civil rights for African Americans would remain at the centre of the American experience for decade upon decade to come.

APPENDIX: PRIMARY SOURCE DOCUMENTS

STEPHEN A. DOUGLAS: DEFENSE OF THE KANSAS-NEBRASKA BILL (1854)

Source: *Appendix to the Congressional Globe*, 33 Cong., 1 Sess., pp. 275–280.

Mr. President, when I proposed on Tuesday last that the Senate should proceed to the consideration of the bill to organize the territories of Nebraska and Kansas ... I desired to refer to two points: first, as to those provisions relating to the Indians; and second, to those which might be supposed to bear upon the question of slavery. ...

Sir, this is all that I intended to say if the question had been taken up for consideration on Tuesday last; but since that time occurrences have transpired which compel me to go more fully into the discussion. It will be borne in mind that the senator from Ohio [Mr. Chase] then objected to the consideration of the bill and asked for its postponement until this day, on the ground that there had not been time to understand and consider its provisions; and the senator from Massachusetts [Mr. Sumner] suggested that the postponement should be for one week, for that purpose. These suggestions seeming to be reasonable to senators around me, I yielded to their request and consented to the postponement of the bill until this day.

Sir, little did I suppose at the time that I granted that act of courtesy to those two senators that they had drafted and published to the world a document, over their own signatures, in which they arraigned me as having been guilty of a criminal betrayal of my trust, as having been guilty of an act of bad faith, and been engaged in an atrocious plot against the cause of free government. Little did I suppose that those two senators had been guilty of such conduct when they called upon me to grant that courtesy, to give them an opportunity of investigating the substitute reported from the committee.

I have since discovered that on that very morning the *National Era*, the Abolition organ in this city, contained an address, signed by certain Abolition confederates, to the people, in which the bill is grossly misrepresented, in which the action of the members of the committee is grossly falsified, in which our motives are arraigned and our characters calumniated. ...

The argument of this manifesto is predicated upon the assumption that the policy of the fathers of the republic was to prohibit slavery in all the territory ceded by the old states to the Union and made United States territory for the purpose of being organized into new states. I take issue upon that statement. Such was not the practice in the early history of the government. It is true that in the territory northwest of the Ohio River slavery was prohibited by the Ordinance of 1787; but it is also true that in the territory south of the Ohio River, to wit, the territory of Tennessee, slavery was permitted and protected; and it is also true that in the organization of the territory of Mississippi, in 1798, the provisions of the Ordinance of 1787 were applied to it, with the exception of Article 6, which prohibited slavery.

Then, sir, you find upon the statute books under Washington and the early Presidents provisions of law showing that in the southwestern territories the right to hold slaves was clearly implied or recognized, while in the northwest territories it was prohibited. The only conclusion that can be fairly and honestly drawn from that legislation is that it was the policy of the fathers of the republic to prescribe a line of demarcation between free territories and slaveholding territories by a natural or a geographical line, being sure to make that line correspond, as near as might be, to the laws of climate, of production, and probably of all those other causes that would control the institution and make it either desirable or undesirable to the people inhabiting the respective territories. ...

A senator from my state, Mr. Jesse B. Thomas, introduced an amendment, known as Section 8 of the bill, in which it was provided that slavery should be prohibited north of 36°30' north latitude, in all that country which we had acquired from France. What was the object of the enactment of Section 8? Was it not to go back to the original policy of prescribing boundaries to the limitation

of free institutions and of slave institutions by a geographical line, in order to avoid all controversy in Congress upon the subject? Hence they extended that geographical line through all the territory purchased from France, which was as far as our possessions then reached. It was not simply to settle the question on that piece of country but it was to carry out a great principle, by extending that dividing line as far west as our territory went, and running it onward on each new acquisition of territory. True, the express enactment of Section 8 of the Missouri Act, now called the Missouri Compromise act, only covered the territory acquired from France; but the principles of the act, the objects of its adoption, the reasons in its support required that it should be extended indefinitely westward, so far as our territory might go, whenever new purchases should be made. ...

Then, sir, in 1848, we acquired from Mexico the country between the Rio Del Norte and the Pacific Ocean. Immediately after that acquisition, the Senate, on my own motion, voted into a bill a provision to extend the Missouri Compromise indefinitely westward to the Pacific Ocean, in the same sense and with the same understanding with which it was originally adopted. That provision passed this body by a decided majority—I think by ten at least—and went to the House of Representatives, and was there defeated by Northern votes.

Now, sir, let us pause and consider for a moment. The first time that the principles of the Missouri Compromise were ever abandoned, the first time they were ever rejected by Congress, was by the defeat of that provision in the House of Representatives in 1848. By whom was that defeat effected? By Northern votes, with Free-Soil proclivities. It was the defeat of that Missouri Compromise that reopened the slavery agitation with all its fury. It was the defeat of that Missouri Compromise that created the tremendous struggle of 1850. It was the defeat of that Missouri Compromise that created the necessity for making a new compromise in 1850. Had we been faithful to the principles of the Missouri Compromise in 1848, this question would not have arisen.

Who was it that was faithless? I undertake to say it was the very men who now insist that the Missouri Compromise was a solemn compact and should never be violated or departed from. Every man who is now assailing the principle of the bill under consideration, so far as I am advised, was opposed to the Missouri Compromise in 1848. The very men who now arraign me for a departure from the Missouri Compromise are the men who successfully violated it, repudiated it, and caused it to be superseded by the compromise measures of 1850. Sir, it is with rather bad grace that the men who proved false themselves should charge upon me and others who were ever faithful the responsibilities and consequences of their own treachery.

Then, sir, as I before remarked, the defeat of the Missouri Compromise in 1848 having created the necessity for the establishment of a new one in 1850, let us see what that compromise was.

The leading feature of the compromise of 1850 was congressional nonintervention as to slavery in the territories; that the people of the territories, and of all the states, were to be allowed to do as they pleased upon the subject of slavery, subject only to the provisions of the Constitution of the United States. That, sir, was the leading feature of the compromise measures of 1850.

Those measures, therefore, abandoned the idea of a geographical line as the boundary between free states and slave states; abandoned it because compelled to do it from an inability to maintain it; and, in lieu of that, substituted a great principle of self-government which would allow the people to do as they thought proper. Now, the question is, when that new compromise, resting upon that great fundamental principle of freedom, was established, was it not an abandonment of the old one—the geographical line? Was it not a supersedure of the old one within the very language of the substitute for the bill which is now under consideration? I say it did supersede it, because it applied its provisions as well to the north as to the south of 36°30′. It established a principle which was equally applicable to the country north as well as south of the parallel of 36°30′—a principle of universal application. …

I am now dealing with the truth and veracity of a combination of men who have assembled in secret caucus upon the Sabbath Day to arraign my conduct and belie my character. I say, therefore, that their manifesto is a slander ... for it says that the Missouri Compromise was not superseded by the measures of 1850, and then it says that the same words in my bill do repeal and annul it. They must be adjudged guilty of one falsehood in order to sustain the other assertion. ...

Sir, this misrepresentation and falsification does not stop here. In order to give greater plausibility to their statement, they go further and state that:

> it is solemnly declared, in the very compromise acts, "that nothing herein contained shall be construed to impair or qualify" the prohibition of slavery north of 36°30'; and yet, in the face of this declaration, that sacred prohibition is said to be overthrown. Can presumption go further?

In the very teeth of the statute, saying that they should come in with or without slavery as they pleased, these men declare that it is stated that it should be forever prohibited. I repeat to them, "Could presumption go further?" Not only presumption in making these statements but the presumption that they could avoid the exposure of their conduct.

In order to give greater plausibility to this falsification of the terms of the compromise measures of 1850, the confederates also declare in their manifesto that they (the territorial bills for the organization of Utah and New Mexico) "applied to the territory acquired from Mexico, and to that only. They were intended as a settlement of the controversy growing out of that acquisition, and of that controversy only. They must stand or fall by their own merits."

I submit to the Senate if there is an intelligent man in America who does not know that that declaration is falsified by the statute from which they quoted? They say that the provisions of that bill were confined to the territory acquired from Mexico, when the very section of the law from which they quoted that proviso did purchase a part of that very territory from the state of Texas. And the next section of the law included that territory in the new territory of Mexico. It took a small portion, also, of the old Louisiana Purchase, and added that to the new territory of Mexico, and made up the rest out of the Mexican acquisitions.

Then, sir, your statutes show, when applied to the map of the country, that the territory of New Mexico was composed of territory acquired from Mexico ... also of territory acquired from Texas, and of territory acquired from France; and yet, in defiance of that statute and in falsification of its terms, we are told, in order to deceive the people, that the bills were confined to the purchase made from Mexico alone; and in order to give it greater solemnity, as was necessary while uttering a falsehood, they repeat it twice, fearing that it would not be believed the first time. What is more, the territory of Utah was not confined to the country acquired from Mexico. That territory, as is well known to every man who understands the geography of the country, includes a large tract of rich and fertile country acquired from France in 1803, and to which Section 8 of the Missouri Act applied in 1820. If these confederates do not know to what country I allude, I only reply that they should have known before they uttered a falsehood and imputed a crime to me.

But I will tell you to what country I allude. By the treaty of 1819, by which we acquired Florida, and fixed a boundary between the United States and Mexico, the boundary was made of the Arkansas River to its source, and then the line ran due north of the source of the Arkansas to the 42nd parallel, then along on the 42nd parallel to the Pacific Ocean. That line, due north from the head of the Arkansas, leaves the whole Middle Park, described in such glowing terms by Colonel Frémont, to the east of the line, and hence a part of the Louisiana Purchase. Yet, inasmuch as that Middle Park is watered and drained by the waters flowing into the Colorado, when we formed the territorial limits of Utah, instead of running that air line, we ran along the ridge of the mountains and cut off that part from Nebraska, or from the Louisiana Purchase, and included it within the limits of the territory of Utah.

Why did we do it? Because we sought for a national boundary; and it was more natural to take the mountains as a boundary than by an air line to cut the valleys on one side of the mountains, and annex them to the country on the other side. And why did we take these natural boundaries, setting at defiance the old boundaries? The simple reason was that so long as we acted upon the principle of settling the slave question by a geographical line, so long we observed those boundaries strictly and rigidly; but when that was abandoned, in consequence of the action of Free-Soilers and Abolitionists—when it was superseded by the compromise measures of 1850, which rested upon a great universal principle— there was no necessity for keeping in view the old and unnatural boundary. For that reason, in making the new territories, we formed natural boundaries, irrespective of the source whence our title was derived. In writing these bills I paid no attention to the fact whether the title was acquired from Louisiana, from France, or from Mexico; for what difference did it make? The principle which we had established in the bill would apply equally well to either. ...

Mr. President ... so far as the question of slavery is concerned, there is nothing in the bill under consideration which does not carry out the principle of the compromise measures of 1850, by leaving the people to do as they please, subject only to the provisions of the Constitution of the United States. If that principle is wrong, the bill is wrong. If that principle is right, the bill is right. It is unnecessary to quibble about phraseology or words; it is not the mere words, the mere phraseology, that our constituents wish to judge by. They wish to know the legal effect of our legislation.

The legal effect of this bill, if it be passed as reported by the Committee on Territories, is neither to legislate slavery into these territories nor out of them, but to leave the people do as they please, under the provisions and subject to the limitations of the Constitution of the United States. Why should not this principle prevail? Why should any man, North or South, object to it? I will especially address the argument to my own section of country, and ask why should any Northern man object to this principle? If you will review the history of the slavery question in the United States, you will see that all the great results in behalf of free institutions which have been worked out have been accomplished by the operation of this principle, and by it alone. ...

Under the operation of this principle, New Hampshire became free, while South Carolina continued to hold slaves; Connecticut abolished slavery, while Georgia held on to it; Rhode Island abandoned the institution, while Maryland preserved it; New York, New Jersey, and Pennsylvania abolished slavery, while Virginia, North Carolina, and Kentucky retained it. Did they do it at your bidding? Did they do it at the dictation of the federal government? Did they do it in obedience to any of your Wilmot Proviso or Ordinances of 1787? Not at all; they did it by virtue of their right as freemen under the Constitution of the United States, to establish and abolish such institutions as they thought their own good required.

Let me ask you where have you succeeded in excluding slavery by an act of Congress from one inch of the American soil? You may tell me that you did it in the Northwest Territory by the Ordinance of 1787. I will show you by the history of the country that you did not accomplish any such thing. You prohibited slavery there by law, but you did not exclude it in fact. Illinois was a part of the Northwest Territory. With the exception of a few French and white settlements, it was a vast wilderness, filled with hostile savages when the Ordinance of 1787 was adopted. Yet, sir, when Illinois was organized into a territorial government, it established and protected slavery, and maintained it in spite of your ordinance and in defiance of its express prohibition. It is a curious fact that so long as Congress said the territory of Illinois should not have slavery, she actually had it; and on the very day when you withdrew your congressional prohibition, the people of Illinois, of their own free will and accord, provided for a system of emancipation. ...

How was it in regard to California? Every one of these Abolition confederates who have thus arraigned me and the Committee on Territories before the country, who have misrepresented our position, and misquoted the law and the fact, predicted that unless Congress interposed by law and prohibited slavery in California, it would inevitably become a slaveholding state. Congress did not interfere; Congress did not prohibit slavery. There was no enactment upon the subject; but the people formed a state constitution and then prohibited slavery. ...

I know of but one territory of the United States where slavery does exist, and that one is where you have prohibited it by law, and it is this very Nebraska Territory. In defiance of Section 8 of the act of 1820, in defiance of congressional dictation, there have been, not many, but a few slaves introduced. ...

I do not like, I never did like, the system of legislation on our part by which a geographical line, in violation of the laws of nature, and climate, and soil, and of the laws of God, should be run to establish institutions for a people; yet, out of a regard for the peace and quiet of the country, out of respect for past pledges, and out of a desire to adhere faithfully to all compromises, I sustained the Missouri Compromise so long as it was in force and advocated its extension to the Pacific. Now, when that has been abandoned, when it has been superseded, when a great principle of self-government has been substituted for it, I choose to cling to that principle and abide in good faith, not only by the letter but by the spirit of the last compromise.

Sir, I do not recognize the right of the Abolitionists of this country to arraign me for being false to sacred pledges, as they have done in their proclamation. Let them show when and where I have ever proposed to violate a compact. I have proved that I stood by the compact of 1820 and 1845, and proposed its continuance and observance in 1848. I have proved that the Free-Soilers and Abolitionists were the guilty parties who violated that compromise then. I should like to compare notes with these Abolition confederates about adherence to compromises. When

did they stand by or approve of any one that was ever made?

Did not every Abolitionist and Free-Soiler in America denounce the Missouri Compromise in 1820? Did they not for years hunt down ravenously for his blood every man who assisted in making that compromise? Did they not in 1845, when Texas was annexed, denounce all of us who went for the annexation of Texas, and for the continuation of the Missouri Compromise line through it? Did they not in 1848 denounce me as a slavery propagandist for standing by the principles of the Missouri Compromise, and proposing to continue the Missouri compromise line to the Pacific Ocean? Did they not themselves violate and repudiate it then? Is not the charge of bad faith true as to every Abolitionist in America, instead of being true as to me and ... those who advocate this bill?

They talk about the bill being a violation of the compromise measures of 1850. Who can show me a man in either house of Congress who was in favor of the compromise measures of 1850, and who is not now in favor of leaving the people of Nebraska and Kansas to do as they please upon the subject of slavery according to the provisions of my bill? Is there one? If so, I have not heard of him. This tornado has been raised by Abolitionists, and Abolitionists alone. They have made an impression upon the public mind in the way in which I have mentioned, by a falsification of the law and the facts; and this whole organization against the compromise measures of 1850 is an

Abolition movement. I presume they had some hope of getting a few tenderfooted Democrats into their plot; and, acting on what they supposed they might do, they sent forth publicly to the world the falsehood that their address was signed by the senators and a majority of the representatives from the state of Ohio; but when we come to examine signatures, we find no one Whig there, no one Democrat there; none but pure, unmitigated, unadulterated Abolitionists. ... Now I ask the friends and the opponents of this measure to look at it as it is. Is not the question involved the simple one, whether the people of the territories shall be allowed to do as they please upon the question of slavery, subject only to the limitations of the Constitution? That is all the bill provides; and it does so in clear, explicit, and unequivocal terms. I know there are some men, Whigs and Democrats, who, not willing to repudiate the Baltimore platform of their own party, would be willing to vote for this principle, provided they could do so in such equivocal terms that they could deny that it means what it was intended to mean in certain localities. I do not wish to deal in any equivocal language. If the principle is right, let it be avowed and maintained. If it is wrong, let it be repudiated. Let all this quibbling about the Missouri Compromise, about the territory acquired from France, about the act of 1820, be cast behind you; for the simple question is—Will you allow the people to legislate for themselves upon the subject of slavery? Why should you not? ...

We intend to stand by the principle of the compromise measures of 1850 ... that principle to which the Democracy are pledged, not merely by the Baltimore platform but by a higher and a more solemn obligation, to which they are pledged by the love and affection which they have for that great fundamental principle of democracy and free institutions which lies at the basis of our creed, and gives every political community the right to govern itself in obedience to the Constitution of the country.

CHARLES SUMNER: THE CRIME AGAINST KANSAS (1856)

Source: *Appendix to the Congressional Globe*, 34 Cong., 1 Sess., pp. 529–544.

It belongs to me now, in the first place, to expose the Crime Against Kansas in its origin and extent. Logically this is the beginning of the argument. I say crime, and deliberately adopt this strongest term as better than any other denoting the consummate transgression. I would go further if language could further go. It is the *crime of crimes*—surpassing far the old *crimen majestatis* [crime against a sovereign power], pursued with vengeance by the laws of Rome, and containing all other crimes, as the greater contains the less. I do not go too far when I call it the *crime against nature*, from which the soul recoils and which language refuses to describe. ...

Sir, the Nebraska Bill was in every respect a swindle. It was a swindle by the

South of the North. It was, on the part of those who had already completely enjoyed their share of the Missouri Compromise, a swindle of those whose share was yet absolutely untouched; and the plea of unconstitutionality set up—like the plea of usury after the borrowed money has been enjoyed—did not make it less a swindle. Urged as a bill of peace, it was a swindle of the whole country. Urged as opening the doors to slave masters with their slaves, it was a swindle of the asserted doctrine of popular sovereignty. Urged as sanctioning popular sovereignty, it was a swindle of the asserted rights of slave masters. It was a swindle of a broad territory, thus cheated of protection against slavery. It was a swindle of a great cause, early espoused by Washington, Franklin, and Jefferson, surrounded by the best fathers of the republic. Sir, it was a swindle of God-given inalienable rights. Turn it over; look at it on all sides, and it is everywhere a swindle; and if the word I now employ has not the authority of classical usage, it has, on this occasion, the indubitable authority of fitness. No other word will adequately express the mingled meanness and wickedness of the cheat.

Its character was still further apparent in the general structure of the bill. Amid overflowing professions of regard for the sovereignty of the people in the territory, they were despoiled of every essential privilege of sovereignty. They were not allowed to choose their governor, secretary, chief justice, associate justices, attorney, or marshal, all of whom are sent from Washington; nor were they allowed to regulate the salaries of any of these functionaries, or the daily allowance of the legislative body, or even the pay of the clerks and doorkeepers; but they were left free to adopt slavery.

And this was called popular sovereignty! Time does not allow, nor does the occasion require that I should stop to dwell on this transparent device to cover a transcendent wrong. Suffice it to say that slavery is in itself an arrogant denial of human rights, and by no human reason can the power to establish such a wrong be placed among the attributes of any just sovereignty. In refusing it such a place I do not deny popular rights, but uphold them; I do not restrain popular rights, but extend them. And, sir, to this conclusion you must yet come unless deaf, not only to the admonitions of political justice but also to the genius of our own Constitution under which, when properly interpreted, no valid claim for slavery can be set up anywhere in the national territory.

The senator from Michigan [Mr. Cass] may say, in response to the senator from Mississippi [Mr. Brown], that slavery cannot go into the territory under the Constitution without legislative introduction; and permit me to add, in response to both, that slavery cannot go there at all. *Nothing can come out of nothing*; and there is absolutely nothing in the Constitution out of which slavery can be derived, while there are provisions which, when properly interpreted, make its existence anywhere within the exclusive national jurisdiction impossible. ...

Mr. President, men are wisely presumed to intend the natural consequences of their conduct, and to seek what their acts seem to promote. Now the Nebraska Bill, on its very face, openly cleared the way for slavery, and it is not wrong to presume that its originators intended the natural consequences of such an act, and sought in this way to extend slavery. Of course they did. And this is the first stage in the Crime Against Kansas. ...

Then was conceived the consummation of the Crime Against Kansas. What could not be accomplished peaceably was to be accomplished forcibly. The reptile monster, that could not be quietly and securely hatched there, was to be pushed full-grown into the territory. All efforts were now given to the dismal work of forcing slavery on free soil. In flagrant derogation of the very popular sovereignty, whose name helped to impose this bill upon the country, the atrocious object was not distinctly avowed. And the avowal has been followed by the act. Slavery has been forcibly introduced into Kansas and placed under the formal safeguards of pretended law. ...

Five several times and more have these invaders entered Kansas in armed array, and thus five several times and more have they trampled upon the organic law of the territory. But these extraordinary expeditions are simply the extraordinary witnesses to successive uninterrupted violence. They stand out conspicuous, but not alone. The spirit of evil, in which they had their origin, was wakeful and incessant. From the beginning, it hung upon the skirts of this interesting territory, harrowing its peace, disturbing its prosperity, and keeping its inhabitants under the painful alarms of war. Thus was all security of person, of property, and of labor overthrown; and when I urge this incontrovertible fact, I set forth a wrong which is small only by the side of the giant wrong for the consummation of which all this was done.

Sir, what is man—what is government—without security; in the absence of which nor man nor government can proceed in development or enjoy the fruits of existence? Without security, civilization is cramped and dwarfed. Without security, there can be no true freedom. Nor shall I say too much when I declare that security, guarded of course by its offspring, freedom, is the true end and aim of government. Of this indispensable boon the people of Kansas have thus far been despoiled—absolutely, totally. All this is aggravated by the nature of their pursuits, rendering them peculiarly sensitive to interruption, and at the same time attesting their innocence.

They are for the most part engaged in the cultivation of the soil, which from time immemorial has been the sweet employment of undisturbed industry. Contented in the returns of bounteous nature and the shade of his own trees, the husbandman is not aggressive. Accustomed to produce and not to destroy, he is essentially peaceful, unless his home is invaded, when his arm derives vigor from the soil he treads and his soul inspiration from the heavens beneath whose canopy he daily toils. And such are the people of Kansas, whose security has been overthrown.

Scenes from which civilization averts her countenance have been a part of their daily life. The border incursions, which, in barbarous ages or barbarous lands, have fretted and harried an exposed people, have been here renewed, with this peculiarity, that our border robbers do not simply levy blackmail and drive off a few cattle like those who acted under the inspiration of the Douglas of other days; that they do not seize a few persons and sweep them away into captivity, like the African slave traders whom we brand as pirates; but that they commit a succession of acts in which all border sorrows and all African wrongs are revived together on American soil, and which, for the time being, annuls all protection of all kinds and enslaves the whole territory.

Private griefs mingle their poignancy with public wrongs. I do not dwell on the anxieties which families have undergone, exposed to sudden assault and obliged to lie down to rest with the alarms of war ringing in their ears, not knowing that another day might be spared to them. Throughout this bitter winter, with the thermometer at 30° below zero, the citizens of Lawrence have been constrained to sleep under arms, with sentinels treading their constant watch against surprise. ...

As every point in a widespread horizon radiates from a common center, so everything said or done in this vast circle of crime radiates from the *one idea*, that Kansas, at all hazards, must be made a slave state. In all the manifold wickednesses that have occurred, and in every successive invasion, this *one idea* has been ever present, as the Satanic tempter—the motive power—the *causing cause*.

To accomplish this result, three things were attempted: first, by outrages of all kinds to drive the friends of freedom already there out of the territory; second, to deter others from coming; and, third, to obtain the complete control of the government. The process of driving out, and also of deterring, has failed. On the contrary, the friends of freedom there became more fixed in their resolves to stay and fight the battle which they had never sought, but from which they disdained to retreat; while the friends of freedom elsewhere were more aroused to the duty of timely succors, by men and munitions of just self-defense.

But, while defeated in the first two processes proposed, the conspirators succeeded in the last. By the violence already portrayed at the election of March 30, when the polls were occupied by the armed hordes from Missouri, they imposed a legislature upon the territory, and thus, under the iron mask of law, established a usurpation not less complete than any in history. ...

Mark, sir, three different legislative enactments which constitute part of this work. First, according to one act, all who deny, by spoken or written word, "the right of persons to hold slaves in this territory" are denounced as felons, to be punished by imprisonment at hard labor for a term not less than two years; it may be for life. And to show the extravagance of this injustice, it has been well put by the senator from Vermont [Mr. Collamer] that should the senator from Michigan [Mr. Cass], who believes that slavery cannot exist in a territory unless introduced by express legislative acts, venture there with his moderate opinions, his doom must be that of a felon! To this extent are the great liberties of speech and of the press subverted.

Second, by another act, entitled "An act concerning attorneys-at-law," no person can practise as an attorney unless he *shall obtain a license* from the territorial courts, which, of course, a tyrannical discretion will be free to deny; and after obtaining such license he is constrained to take an oath, not only "to support" the Constitution of the United States but also "to support and sustain"—mark here the reduplication—the Territorial Act and the Fugitive Slave Bill, thus erecting a test for the function of the bar calculated to exclude citizens who honestly regard that latter legislative enormity as unfit to be obeyed.

And third, by another act, entitled "An act concerning jurors," all persons "conscientiously opposed to holding slaves," or "not admitting the right to hold slaves in the territory," are excluded from the jury on every question, civil or criminal, arising out of asserted slave property; while, in all cases, the summoning of the jury is left without one word of restraint to "the marshal, sheriff, or other officer," who are thus free to pack it according to their tyrannical discretion.

For the ready enforcement of all statutes against human freedom, the President had already furnished a powerful quota of officers in the governor, chief justice, judges, secretary, attorney, and marshal. The legislature completed this part of the work by constituting, in each county, a board of commissioners, composed of two persons, associated with the probate judge, whose duty it is "to appoint a county treasurer, coroner, justices of the peace, constables, and *all* other officers provided for by law," and then proceeded to the choice of this very board; thus delegating and diffusing their usurped power, and tyrannically imposing upon the territory a crowd of officers, in whose appointment the people have had no voice, directly or indirectly.

And still the final, inexorable work remained. A legislature, renovated in both branches, could not assemble until 1858, so that, during this long, intermediate period, this whole system must continue in the likeness of law, unless overturned by the federal government, or, in default of such interposition, by a generous uprising of an oppressed people. But it was necessary to guard against the possibility of change, even tardily, at a future election; and this was done by two different acts; under the first of which, all who will not take the oath to support the Fugitive Slave Bill are excluded from the elective franchise; and under the second of which, all others are entitled to vote who shall tender a tax of $1 to the sheriff on the day of election; thus, by provision of territorial law, disfranchising all opposed to slavery, and at the same time opening the door to the votes of the invaders by an unconstitutional shibboleth, excluding from the polls the mass of actual settlers, and by making the franchise depend upon a petty tax only, admitting to the polls the mass of borderers from Missouri. Thus, by tyrannical forethought, the usurpation not only fortified all that it did but assumed a *self-perpetuating* energy.

Thus was the Crime consummated. Slavery now stands erect, clanking its chains on the territory of Kansas, surrounded by a code of death, and trampling upon all cherished liberties, whether of speech, the press, the bar, the trial by jury, or the electoral franchise. And, sir, all this has been done, not merely to introduce a wrong which in itself is a denial of all rights, and in dread of which a mother has lately taken the life of her offspring; not merely, as has been sometimes said, to protect slavery in Missouri, since it is futile for this state to complain of freedom on the side of Kansas when freedom exists without complaint on the side of Iowa and also on the side of Illinois; but it has been done for the sake of political power, in order to bring two new slaveholding senators upon this floor and thus to fortify in the national government the desperate chances of a waning oligarchy.

As the ship, voyaging on pleasant summer seas, is assailed by a pirate crew and robbed for the sake of its doubloons and dollars—so is this beautiful territory now assailed in its peace and prosperity, and robbed in order to wrest its political power to the side of slavery. Even now the black flag of the land pirates from Missouri waves at the masthead; in their laws you hear the pirate yell and see the flash of the pirate knife; while, incredible to relate, the President, gathering the slave power at his back, testifies a pirate sympathy.

Sir, all this was done in the name of popular sovereignty. And this is the close of the tragedy. Popular sovereignty, which, when truly understood, is a fountain of just power, has ended in popular slavery; not merely in the subjection of the unhappy African race but of this proud Caucasian blood which you boast. The profession with which you began, of *All by the People*, has been lost in the wretched reality of *Nothing for the People*. Popular sovereignty, in whose deceitful name plighted faith was broken and an ancient landmark of freedom was overturned, now lifts itself before us, like sin, in the terrible picture of Milton—

That seemed a woman to the waist, and fair;
But ended foul in many a scaly fold,
Voluminous and vast! a serpent armed
With mortal sting: about her middle round
A cry of hell-hounds never ceasing barked
With wide Cerberian mouths full loud and rung

*A hideous peal: yet, when they list,
would creep,
If aught disturbed their noise,
into her womb,
And kennel there; yet there still
barked, and howled
Within, unseen.*

The image is complete at all points; and, with this exposure, I take my leave of the Crime Against Kansas.

ROGER TANEY: *DRED SCOTT V. SANDFORD* (1857)

Source: *Reports of Cases Argued and Adjudged in the Supreme Court of the United States*, Benjamin C. Howard, ed., Washington, 1857, Vol. 19, pp. 393ff.

Mr. Chief Justice Taney delivered the opinion of the Court. ...

The question is simply this: Can a Negro, whose ancestors were imported into this country and sold as slaves, become a member of the political community formed and brought into existence by the Constitution of the United States, and as such become entitled to all the rights and privileges and immunities, guaranteed by that instrument to the citizen? One of which rights is the privilege of suing in a court of the United States in the cases specified in the Constitution.

It will be observed that the plea applies to that class of persons only whose ancestors were Negroes of the African race and imported into this country, and sold and held as slaves. The only matter in issue before the Court, therefore, is

whether the descendants of such slaves, when they shall be emancipated, or who are born of parents who had become free before their birth, are citizens of a state in the sense in which the word "citizen" is used in the Constitution of the United States. And this being the only matter in dispute on the pleadings, the Court must be understood as speaking in this opinion of that class only; that is, of those persons who are the descendants of Africans who were imported into this country and sold as slaves. ...

In discussing this question, we must not confound the rights of citizenship which a state may confer within its own limits and the rights of citizenship as a member of the Union. It does not by any means follow, because he has all the rights and privileges of a citizen of a state, that he must be a citizen of the United States. He may have all of the rights and privileges of the citizen of a state and yet not be entitled to the rights and privileges of a citizen in any other state. ...

It is true, every person, and every class and description of persons who were at the time of the adoption of the Constitution recognized as citizens in the several states, became also citizens of this new political body; but none other; it was formed by them and for them and their posterity, but for no one else. And the personal rights and privileges guaranteed to citizens of this new sovereignty were intended to embrace those only who were then members of the several state communities or who should afterward by birthright or otherwise become members, according to the provisions of the Constitution and the principles on which it was founded. It was the union of those who were at that time members of distinct and separate political communities into one political family, whose power, for certain specified purposes, was to extend over the whole territory of the United States. And it gave to each citizen rights and privileges outside of his state which he did not before possess, and placed him in every other state upon a perfect equality with its own citizens as to rights of person and rights of property—it made him a citizen of the United States.

It becomes necessary, therefore, to determine who were citizens of the several states when the Constitution was adopted. And, in order to do this, we must recur to the governments and institutions of the thirteen colonies when they separated from Great Britain and formed new sovereignties and took their places in the family of independent nations. We must inquire who, at that time, were recognized as the people or citizens of a state, whose rights and liberties had been outraged by the English government; and who declared their independence and assumed the powers of government to defend their rights by force of arms.

In the opinion of the Court, the legislation and histories of the times, and the language used in the Declaration of Independence, show that neither the class of persons who had been imported as slaves nor their descendants, whether they had become free or not, were then acknowledged as a part of the people nor intended to be included in the general words used in that memorable instrument.

It is difficult at this day to realize the state of public opinion in relation to that unfortunate race which prevailed in the civilized and enlightened portions of the world at the time of the Declaration of Independence and when the Constitution of the United States was framed and adopted. But the public history of every European nation displays it in a manner too plain to be mistaken.

They had for more than a century before been regarded as beings of an inferior order and altogether unfit to associate with the white race, either in social or political relations; and so far inferior that they had no rights which the white man was bound to respect; and that the Negro might justly and lawfully be reduced to slavery for his benefit. He was bought and sold and treated as an ordinary article of merchandise and traffic whenever a profit could be made by it. This opinion was at that time fixed and universal in the civilized portion of the white race. It was regarded as an axiom in morals as well as in politics, which no one thought of disputing, or supposed to be open to dispute; and men in every grade and position in society daily and habitually acted upon it in their private pursuits, as well as in matters of public concern, without doubting for a moment the correctness of this opinion. ...

The language of the Declaration of Independence is equally conclusive. It begins by declaring that:

When, in the course of human events, it becomes necessary for one people to dissolve the political bands which have connected them with another, and to assume among the powers of the earth the separate and equal station to which the laws of nature and nature's God entitle them, a decent respect for the opinions of mankind requires that they should declare the causes which impel them to the separation.

It then proceeds to say:

We hold these truths to be self-evident: that all men are created equal; that they are endowed by their Creator with certain unalienable rights; that among them is life, liberty, and the pursuit of happiness; that to secure these rights, governments are instituted, deriving their just powers from the consent of the governed.

The general words above quoted would seem to embrace the whole human family, and if they were used in a similar instrument at this day would be so understood. But it is too clear for dispute that the enslaved African race were not intended to be included and formed no part of the people who framed and adopted this Declaration; for if the language, as understood in that day, would embrace them, the conduct of the distinguished men who framed the Declaration would have been utterly and flagrantly inconsistent with the principles they asserted; and instead of the sympathy of mankind, to which they so confidently appealed, they would have deserved and received universal rebuke and reprobation.

Yet the men who framed this Declaration were great men—high in literary acquirements, high in their sense of honor and incapable of asserting principles inconsistent with those on which they were acting. They perfectly understood the meaning of the language they used and how it would be understood by others; and they knew that it would not in any part of the civilized world be supposed to embrace the Negro race, which, by common consent, had been excluded from civilized governments and the family of nations and doomed to slavery. They spoke and acted according to the then established doctrines and principles and in the ordinary language of the day, and no one misunderstood them. The unhappy black race were separated from the white by indelible marks, and laws long before established, and were never thought of or spoken of except as property and when the claims of the owner or the profit of the trader were supposed to need protection.

This state of public opinion had undergone no change when the Constitution was adopted, as is equally evident from its provisions and language.

The brief Preamble sets forth by whom it was formed, for what purposes, and for whose benefit and protection. It declares that it is formed by the *people* of the United States; that is to say, by those who were members of the different political communities in the several states; and its great object is declared to be to secure the blessings of liberty to themselves and their posterity. It speaks in general terms of the *people* of the United States and of *citizens* of the several states when it is providing for the exercise of the powers granted or the privileges secured to the citizen. It does not define what description of persons are intended to be included under these terms, or who shall be regarded as a citizen and one of the people. It uses them as terms so well understood that no further description or definition was necessary.

But there are two clauses in the Constitution which point directly and specifically to the Negro race as a separate class of persons and show clearly that they were not regarded as a portion of the people or citizens of the government then formed.

One of these clauses reserves to each of the thirteen states the right to import slaves until the year 1808, if it thinks proper. And the importation which it thus sanctions was unquestionably of persons of the race of which we are speaking, as the traffic in slaves in the United States had always been confined to them. And by the other provision the states pledge themselves to each other to maintain the right of property of the master by delivering up to him any slave who may have escaped from his service and be found within their respective territories.

By the first above mentioned clause, therefore, the right to purchase and hold this property is directly sanctioned and authorized for twenty years by the people who framed the Constitution. And by the second, they pledge themselves to maintain and uphold the right of the master in the manner specified, as long as the government they then formed should endure. And these two provisions show, conclusively, that neither the description of persons therein referred to nor their descendants were embraced in any of the other provisions of the Constitution; for certainly these two clauses were not intended to confer on them or their posterity the blessings of liberty or any of the personal rights so carefully provided for the citizen. ...

Undoubtedly, a person may be a citizen, that is, a member of the community who form the sovereignty, although he exercises no share of the political power and is incapacitated from holding particular offices. Women and minors, who form a part of the political family, cannot vote; and when a property qualification is required to vote or hold a particular office, those who have not the necessary qualification cannot vote or hold the office, yet they are citizens.

So, too, a person may be entitled to vote by the law of the state who is not a citizen even of the state itself. And in some of the states of the Union foreigners not naturalized are allowed to vote. And the state may give the right to free Negroes and mulattoes, but that does not make them citizens of the state, and still less of the United States. And the provision in the Constitution giving privileges and immunities in other states does not apply to them.

Neither does it apply to a person who, being the citizen of a state, migrates to another state; for then he becomes subject to the laws of the state in which he lives and he is no longer a citizen of the state from which he removed. And the state in which he resides may then, unquestionably, determine his *status* or condition and place him among the class of persons who are not recognized as citizens but belong to an inferior and subject race; and may deny him the privileges and immunities enjoyed by its citizens.

But so far as mere rights of person are concerned, the provision in question is confined to citizens of a state who are temporarily in another state without taking up their residence there. It gives them no political rights in the state as to voting or holding office, or in any other respect; for a citizen of one state has no right to participate in the government of another. But if he ranks as a citizen in the state to which he belongs, within the meaning of the Constitution of the United States, then, whenever he goes into another state, the Constitution clothes him, as to the rights of person, with all the privileges and immunities which belong to citizens of the state.

And if persons of the African race are citizens of a state, and of the United States, they would be entitled to all of these privileges and immunities in every state, and the state could not restrict them; for they would hold these privileges and immunities under the paramount authority of the federal government, and its courts would be bound to maintain and enforce them, the Constitution and laws of the state to the contrary notwithstanding. And if the states could limit or restrict them, or place the party in an inferior grade, this clause of the Constitution would be unmeaning and could have no operation; and would give no rights to the citizen when in another state. He would have none but what the state itself chose to allow him.

This is evidently not the construction or meaning of the clause in question. It guarantees rights to the citizen, and the state cannot withhold them. And these rights are of a character and would lead to consequences which make it absolutely certain that the African race were not included under the name of citizens of a state and were not in the contemplation of the framers of the Constitution when these privileges and immunities were provided for the protection of the citizen in other states. ...

No one, we presume, supposes that any change in public opinion or feeling in relation to this unfortunate race, in the civilized nations of Europe or in this country, should induce the Court to give to the words of the Constitution a more liberal construction in their favor than they were intended to bear when the instrument was framed and adopted. Such an argument would be altogether inadmissible in any tribunal called on to interpret it. If any of its provisions are deemed unjust, there is a mode prescribed in the instrument itself by which it may be amended; but, while it remains unaltered, it must be construed now as it was understood at the time of its adoption.

It is not only the same in words but the same in meaning and delegates, the same powers to the government and reserves, and secures the same rights and privileges to the citizen; and, as long as it continues to exist in its present form, it speaks not only in the same words but with the same meaning and intent with which it spoke when it came from the hands of its framers and was voted on and adopted by the people of the United States. Any other rule of construction would abrogate the judicial character of this Court and make it the mere reflex of the popular opinion or passion of the day. This Court was not created by the Constitution for such purposes. Higher and graver trusts have been confided to it and it must not falter in the path of duty.

What the construction was at that time, we think, can hardly admit of doubt. We have the language of the Declaration of Independence and of the Articles of Confederation, in addition to the plain words of the Constitution itself; we have the legislation of the different states before, about the time, and since the Constitution was adopted; we have the legislation of Congress, from the time of its adoption to a recent period; and we have the constant and uniform action of the Executive Department, all concurring together and leading to the same result. And, if anything in relation to the construction of the Constitution can be regarded as settled, it is that which we now give to the word "citizen" and the word "people."

And upon a full and careful consideration of the subject, the Court is of opinion that, upon the facts stated in the plea in abatement, Dred Scott was not a citizen of Missouri within the meaning of the Constitution of the United States and not entitled as such to sue in its courts, and, consequently, that the Circuit Court had no jurisdiction of the case and that the judgment on the plea in abatement is erroneous. ...

ABRAHAM LINCOLN: "A HOUSE DIVIDED" (1858)

Source: *Political Speeches and Debates of Abraham Lincoln and Stephen A. Douglas 1854–1861*, Alonzo T. Jones, ed., Battle Creek, Mich., 1895, pp. 52–74.

Mr. President and Gentlemen of the Convention:

If we could first know where we are and whither we are tending, we could better judge what to do and how to do it. We are now far into the fifth year since a policy was initiated with the avowed object and confident promise of putting an end to slavery agitation. Under the operation of that policy, that agitation has not only not ceased but has constantly augmented. In my opinion, it will not cease until a crisis shall have been reached and passed. "A house divided against itself cannot stand." I believe this government cannot endure, permanently, half slave and half free. I do not expect the Union to be dissolved; I do not expect the house to fall; but I do expect it will cease to be divided. It will become all one thing, or all the other. Either the opponents of slavery will arrest the further spread of it and place it where the public mind shall rest in the belief that it is in the course of ultimate extinction, or its advocates will push it forward till it shall become alike lawful in all the states, old as well as new, North as well as South.

Have we no tendency to the latter condition?

Let anyone who doubts carefully contemplate that now almost complete legal combination—piece of machinery, so to speak—compounded of the Nebraska doctrine and the *Dred Scott* decision. Let him consider, not only what work the machinery is adapted to do, and how well adapted, but also let him study the history of its construction and trace, if he can, or rather fail, if he can, to trace the evidences of design and concert of action among its chief architects, from the beginning.

The new year of 1854 found slavery excluded from more than half the states by state constitutions and from most of the national territory by congressional prohibition. Four days later commenced the struggle which ended in repealing that congressional prohibition. This opened all the national territory to slavery and was the first point gained.

But, so far, Congress *only* had acted; and an endorsement by the people, real or apparent, was indispensable to save the point already gained and give chance for more.

This necessity had not been overlooked, but had been provided for, as well as might be, in the notable argument of "squatter sovereignty," otherwise called "sacred right of self-government," which latter phrase, though expressive of the only rightful basis of any government, was so perverted in this attempted use of it as to amount to just this: That if any *one* man choose to enslave *another*, no *third* man shall be allowed to object. That argument was incorporated into the Nebraska Bill itself, in the language which follows:

> *It being the true intent and meaning of this act not to legislate slavery into any territory or state, nor to exclude it therefrom, but to leave the people thereof perfectly free to form and regulate their domestic institutions in their own way, subject only to the Constitution of the United States.*

Then opened the roar of loose declamation in favor of "squatter sovereignty" and "sacred right of self-government." "But," said opposition members, "let us amend the bill so as to expressly declare that the people of the territory may exclude slavery." "Not we," said the friends of the measure; and down they voted the amendment.

While the Nebraska Bill was passing through Congress, a law case, involving the question of a Negro's freedom, by reason of his owner having voluntarily taken him first into a free state and then into a territory covered by the congressional prohibition, and held him as a slave for a long time in each, was passing through the United States Circuit Court for the district of Missouri; and both Nebraska Bill and lawsuit were brought to a decision in the same month of May 1854. The Negro's name was Dred Scott, which name now designates the decision finally made in the case. Before the then next presidential election, the law case came to, and was argued in, the Supreme Court of the United States; but the decision of it was deferred until after the election. Still, before the election, Senator Trumbull, on the floor of the Senate, requested the leading advocate of the Nebraska Bill to state his opinion whether the people of a territory can constitutionally exclude slavery from their limits; and the latter answers: "That is a question for the Supreme Court."

The election came. Mr. Buchanan was elected, and the endorsement, such as it was, secured. That was the second point gained. The endorsement, however, fell short of a clear popular majority by nearly 400,000 votes, and so, perhaps, was not overwhelmingly reliable and satisfactory. The outgoing President, in his last annual message, as impressively as possible echoed back upon the people the weight and authority of the endorsement. The Supreme Court met again, did not announce their decision, but ordered a reargument.

The presidential inauguration came, and still no decision of the Court; but the incoming President, in his inaugural address, fervently exhorted the people to abide by the forthcoming decision, whatever it might be. Then, in a few days, came the decision.

The reputed author of the Nebraska Bill finds an early occasion to make a speech at this capital endorsing the *Dred Scott* decision, and vehemently denouncing all opposition to it. The new President, too, seizes the early occasion of the Silliman letter to endorse and strongly construe that decision, and to express his astonishment that any different view had ever been entertained!

At length a squabble springs up between the President and the author of the Nebraska Bill, on the mere question of *fact*, whether the Lecompton constitution was or was not in any just sense made by the people of Kansas; and in that quarrel the latter declares that all he wants is a fair vote for the people, and that he cares not whether slavery be voted *down* or voted *up*. I do not understand his declaration, that he cares not whether slavery be voted down or voted up, to be intended by him other than as an apt definition of the policy he would impress upon the public mind—the principle for which he declares he has suffered so much and is ready to suffer to the end. And well may he cling to that principle! If he has any parental feeling, well may he cling to it. That principle is the only shred left of his original Nebraska doctrine.

Under the *Dred Scott* decision, "squatter sovereignty" squatted out of existence, tumbled down like temporary scaffolding; like the mold at the foundry, served through one blast and fell back into loose sand; helped to carry an election and then was kicked to the winds. His late joint struggle with the Republicans against the Lecompton constitution involves nothing of the original Nebraska doctrine. That struggle was made on a point—the right of a people to make their own constitution—upon which he and the Republicans have never differed.

The several points of the *Dred Scott* decision, in connection with Senator Douglas' "care not" policy, constitute the piece of machinery in its present state of advancement. This was the third point gained. The working points of that machinery are:

First, that no Negro slave, imported as such from Africa, and no descendant of such slave can ever be a citizen of any state in the sense of that term as used in the Constitution of the United States. This point is made in order to deprive the Negro, in every possible event, of the benefit of that provision of the United States Constitution which declares that "the citizens of each state shall be entitled to all the privileges and immunities of citizens in the several states."

Second, that, "subject to the Constitution of the United States," neither Congress nor a territorial legislature can exclude slavery from any United States territory. This point is made in order that individual men may fill up the territories with slaves, without danger of losing them as property, and thus enhance the chances of permanency to the institution through all the future.

Third, that whether the holding a Negro in actual slavery in a free state makes him free, as against the holder, the United States courts will not decide, but will leave to be decided by the courts of any slave state the Negro may be forced into by the master. This point is made, not to be pressed immediately but, if acquiesced in for awhile, and apparently endorsed by the people at an election, then to sustain the logical conclusion that what Dred Scott's master might lawfully do with Dred Scott in the free state of Illinois, every other master may lawfully do with any other one, or 1,000 slaves, in Illinois or in any other free state.

Auxiliary to all this, and working hand in hand with it, the Nebraska doctrine, or what is left of it, is to educate and mold public opinion, at least Northern public opinion, not to care whether slavery is voted down or voted up. This shows exactly where we now are; and partially, also, whither we are tending.

It will throw additional light on the latter to go back and run the mind over the string of historical facts already stated. Several things will now appear less dark and mysterious than they did when they were transpiring. The people were to be left "perfectly free," "subject only to the Constitution." What the Constitution had to do with it, outsiders could not then see. Plainly enough, now, it was an exactly fitted niche for the *Dred Scott* decision to afterward come in and declare the perfect freedom of the people to be just no freedom at all.

Why was the amendment expressly declaring the right of the people voted down? Plainly enough, now, the adoption of it would have spoiled the niche for the *Dred Scott* decision. Why was the Court decision held up? Why even a senator's individual opinion withheld till after the presidential election? Plainly enough, now, the speaking out then would have damaged the "perfectly free" argument upon which the election was to be carried. Why the outgoing President's felicitation on the endorsement? Why the delay of a reargument? Why the incoming President's advance exhortation in favor of the decision? These things look like the cautious patting and petting of a spirited horse preparatory to mounting him when it is dreaded that he may give the rider a fall. And why the hasty after-endorsement of the decision by the President and others?

We cannot absolutely know that all these exact adaptations are the result of preconcert. But when we see a lot of framed timbers, different portions of which we know have been gotten out at different times and places and by different workmen—Stephen, Franklin, Roger, and James, for instance—and when we see these timbers joined together and see they exactly make the frame of a house or a mill, all the tenons and mortises exactly fitting, and all the lengths and proportions of the different pieces exactly adapted to their respective places, and not a piece too many or too few, not omitting even scaffolding, or, if a single piece be lacking, we see the place in the frame exactly fitted and prepared yet to bring such piece in—in such a case, we find it impossible not to believe that Stephen and Franklin and Roger and James all understood one another from the beginning, and all worked upon a common plan or draft drawn up before the first blow was struck.

HENRY DAVID THOREAU: A PLEA FOR CAPTAIN JOHN BROWN (1859)

Source: *Echoes of Harper's Ferry*, James Redpath, ed., Boston, 1860.

I trust that you will pardon me for being here. I do not wish to force my thoughts upon you, but I feel forced myself. Little as I know of Captain Brown, I would fain do my part to correct the tone and the statements of the newspapers, and of my countrymen generally, respecting his character and actions. It costs us nothing to be just. We can at least express our sympathy with and admiration of him and his companions, and that is what I now propose to do. ...

When the troubles in Kansas began, he sent several of his sons thither to strengthen the party of the free state men, fitting them out with such weapons as he had; telling them that if the troubles should increase and there should be need of him, he would follow to assist them with his hand and counsel. This, as you all know, he soon after did; and it was through his agency, far more than any other's, that Kansas was made free. ...

I should say that he was an old-fashioned man in his respect for the

Constitution and his faith in the permanence of this Union. Slavery he deemed to be wholly opposed to these, and he was its determined foe.

He was by descent and birth a New England farmer, a man of great common sense, deliberate and practical as that class is, and tenfold more so. He was like the best of those who stood at Concord Bridge once, on Lexington Common, and on Bunker Hill, only he was firmer and higher principled than any that I have chanced to hear of as there. It was no Abolition lecturer that converted him. Ethan Allen and Stark, with whom he may in some respects be compared, were rangers in a lower and less important field. They could bravely face their country's foes, but he had the courage to face his country herself when she was in the wrong. A Western writer says, to account for his escape from so many perils, that he was concealed under a "rural exterior"; as if, in that prairie land, a hero should, by good rights, wear a citizen's dress only.

He did not go to the college called Harvard, good old Alma Mater as she is. He was not fed on the pap that is there furnished. As he phrased it, "I know no more of grammar than one of your calves." But he went to the great university of the West, where he sedulously pursued the study of liberty, for which he had early betrayed a fondness, and, having taken many degrees, he finally commenced the public practice of humanity in Kansas, as you all know. Such were *his humanities*, and not any study of grammar. He would have left

a Greek accent slanting the wrong way and righted up a falling man.

He was one of that class of whom we hear a great deal, but, for the most part, see nothing at all—the Puritans. It would be in vain to kill him. He died lately in the time of Cromwell, but he reappeared here. Why should he not? Some of the Puritan stock are said to have come over and settled in New England. They were a class that did something else than celebrate their forefathers' day and eat parched corn in remembrance of that time. They were neither Democrats nor Republicans but men of simple habits, straightforward, prayerful; not thinking much of rulers who did not fear God, not making many compromises, nor seeking after available candidates. ...

He was never able to find more than a score or so of recruits whom he would accept, and only about a dozen, among them his sons, in whom he had perfect faith. When he was here, some years ago, he showed to a few a little manuscript book—his "orderly book," I think he called it—containing the names of his company in Kansas and the rules by which they bound themselves; and he stated that several of them had already sealed the contract with their blood. When someone remarked that, with the addition of a chaplain, it would have been a perfect Cromwellian troop, he observed that he would have been glad to add a chaplain to the list if he could have found one who could fill that office worthily. It is easy enough to find one for the United States Army. I believe that he had prayers in his camp morning and evening, nevertheless.

He was a man of Spartan habits, and at sixty was scrupulous about his diet at your table, excusing himself by saying that he must eat sparingly and fare hard as became a soldier or one who was fitting himself for difficult enterprises, a life of exposure.

A man of rare common sense and directness of speech, as of action; a Transcendentalist above all, a man of ideas and principles—that was what distinguished him—not yielding to a whim or transient impulse but carrying out the purpose of a life. I noticed that he did not overstate anything but spoke within bounds. I remember, particularly, how, in his speech here, he referred to what his family had suffered in Kansas, without ever giving the least vent to his pent-up fire. It was a volcano with an ordinary chimney flue. Also referring to the deeds of certain border ruffians, he said, rapidly paring away his speech, like an experienced soldier, keeping a reserve of force and meaning, "They had a perfect right to be hung."

He was not in the least a rhetorician, was not talking to Buncombe or his constituents anywhere, had no need to invent anything but to tell the simple truth and communicate his own resolution; therefore, he appeared incomparably strong, and eloquence in Congress and elsewhere seemed to me at a discount. It was like the speeches of Cromwell compared with those of an ordinary king. ...

As for his recent failure, we do not know the facts about it. It was evidently far from being a wild and desperate attempt. His enemy Mr. Vallandigham is compelled to say that "it was among the best planned and executed conspiracies that ever failed."

Not to mention his other successes, was it a failure, or did it show a want of good management, to deliver from bondage a dozen human beings and walk off with them by broad daylight, for weeks if not months, at a leisurely pace, through one state after another for half the length of the North, conspicuous to all parties, with a price set upon his head, going into a courtroom on his way and telling what he had done, thus convincing Missouri that it was not profitable to try to hold slaves in his neighborhood? And this, not because the government menials were lenient but because they were afraid of him.

Yet he did not attribute his success, foolishly, to "his star" or to any magic. He said, truly, that the reason why such greatly superior numbers quailed before him was, as one of his prisoners confessed, because they *lacked a cause*—a kind of armor which he and his party never lacked. When the time came, few men were found willing to lay down their lives in defense of what they knew to be wrong; they did not like that this should be their last act in this world.

But to make haste to *his* last act and its effects.

The newspapers seem to ignore, or perhaps are really ignorant of the fact, that there are at least as many as two or three individuals to a town throughout the North who think much as the present speaker does about him and his enterprise. I do not hesitate to say that they are an important and growing party. We aspire to be something more than stupid and timid chattels, pretending to read history and our Bibles, but desecrating every house and every day we breathe in. Perhaps anxious politicians may prove that only seventeen white men and five Negroes were concerned in the late enterprise; but their very anxiety to prove this might suggest to themselves that all is not told.

Why do they still dodge the truth? They are so anxious because of a dim consciousness of the fact, which they do not distinctly face, that at least a million of the free inhabitants of the United States would have rejoiced if it had succeeded. They at most only criticize the tactics. Though we wear no crepe, the thought of that man's position and probable fate is spoiling many a man's day here at the North for other thinking. If anyone who has seen him here can pursue successfully any other train of thought, I do not know what he is made of. If there is any such who gets his usual allowance of sleep, I will warrant him to fatten easily under any circumstances which do not touch his body or purse. I put a piece of paper and a pencil under my pillow, and when I could not sleep, I wrote in the dark.

On the whole, my respect for my fellowmen, except as one may outweigh a million, is not being increased these days. I have noticed the cold-blooded way in which newspaper writers and men generally speak of this event, as if an ordinary malefactor, though one of unusual "pluck"—as the governor of Virginia is reported to have said, using the language of the cockpit, "the gamest man he ever saw"—had been caught and were about to be hung. He was not dreaming of his foes when the governor thought he looked so brave. It turns what sweetness I have to gall to hear, or hear of, the remarks of some of my neighbors.

When we heard at first that he was dead, one of my townsmen observed that "he died as the fool dieth"; which, pardon me, for an instant suggested a likeness in him dying to my neighbor living. Others, craven-hearted, said disparagingly, that "he threw his life away," because he resisted the government. Which way have they thrown *their* lives, pray? such as would praise a man for attacking singly an ordinary band of thieves or murderers. I hear another ask, Yankee-like, "What will he gain by it?" as if he expected to fill his pockets by this enterprise. Such a one has no idea of gain but in this worldly sense. If it does not lead to a "surprise" party, if he does not get a new pair of boots, or a vote of thanks, it must be a failure. "But he won't gain anything by it."

Well, no, I don't suppose he could get four-and-sixpence a day for being hung, take the year round; but then he stands a chance to save a considerable part of his soul—and *such* a soul!—when *you* do not. No doubt you can get more in your market for a quart of milk than for a quart of blood, but that is not the market that heroes carry their blood to. Such do not know that like the seed is the fruit and that, in the moral world, when good seed is planted good fruit is inevitable and does not depend on our watering and cultivating; that when you plant, or bury, a hero in his field, a crop of heroes is sure to spring up. This is a seed of such force and vitality, that it does not ask our leave to germinate. ...

The modern Christian is a man who has consented to say all the prayers in the liturgy, provided you will let him go straight to bed and sleep quietly afterward. All his prayers begin with "Now I lay me down to sleep," and he is forever looking forward to the time when he shall go to his *"long* rest." He has consented to perform certain old, established charities, too, after a fashion, but he does not wish to hear of any new-fangled ones; he doesn't wish to have any supplementary articles added to the contract to fit it to the present time. He shows the whites of his eyes on the Sabbath, and the blacks all the rest of the week.

The evil is not merely a stagnation of blood but a stagnation of spirit. Many, no doubt, are well-disposed but sluggish by constitution and by habit, and they cannot conceive of a man who is actuated by higher motives than they are. Accordingly, they pronounce this man insane, for they know that *they* could never act as he does as long as they were themselves. ...

I read all the newspapers I could get within a week after this event, and I do not remember in them a single expression of sympathy for these men. I have since seen one noble statement, in a Boston paper, not editorial. Some voluminous sheets decided not to print the full report of Brown's words to the exclusion of other matter. It was as if a publisher should reject the manuscript of the New Testament and print Wilson's last speech. The same journal which contained this pregnant news was chiefly filled, in parallel columns, with the reports of the political conventions that were being held. But the descent to them was too steep. They should have been spared this contrast, been printed in an extra at least.

To turn from the voices and deeds of earnest men to the *cackling* of political conventions! Office seekers and speechmakers who do not so much as lay an honest egg but wear their breasts bare upon an egg of chalk! Their great game is the game of straws, or rather that universal aboriginal game of the platter, at which the Indians cried *hub, bub*! Exclude the reports of religious and political conventions and publish the words of a living man.

But I object not so much to what they have omitted as to what they have inserted. Even the *Liberator* called it "a misguided, wild, and apparently insane — effort." As for the herd of newspapers and magazines, I do not chance to know an editor in the country who will deliberately print anything which he knows will ultimately and permanently reduce the number of his subscribers. They do not believe that it would be expedient. How then can they print truth? If we do not say pleasant things, they argue, nobody will attend to us. And so they do like some traveling auctioneers, who sing an obscene song in order to draw a crowd around them.

Republican editors, obliged to get their sentences ready for the morning edition and accustomed to look at everything by the twilight of politics, express no admiration, nor true sorrow even, but call these men "deluded fanatics," "mistaken men"—"insane" or "crazed." It suggests what a *sane* set of editors we are blessed with, *not* "mistaken men"; who know very well on which side their bread is buttered, at least.

A man does a brave and humane deed, and at once, on all sides, we hear people and parties declaring, "I didn't do it, nor countenance *him* to do it, in any conceivable way. It can't be fairly inferred from my past career." I, for one, am not interested to hear you define your position. I don't know that I ever was or ever shall be. I think it is mere egotism or impertinent at this time. Ye needn't take so much pains to wash your skirts of him. No intelligent man will ever be convinced that he was any creature of yours. He went and came, as he himself informs us, "under the auspices of John Brown and nobody else." The Republican Party does not perceive how many his *failure* will make to vote more correctly than they would have them. They have counted the votes of Pennsylvania & Co., but they have not correctly counted Captain Brown's vote. He has taken the wind out of their sails, the little wind they had, and they may as well lie to and repair. ...

The slave ship is on her way, crowded with its dying victims; new cargoes are being added in midocean; a small crew of slaveholders, countenanced by a large body of passengers, is smothering 4 million under the hatches; and yet the politician asserts that the only proper way by which deliverance is to be obtained is by "the quiet diffusion of the sentiments of humanity," without any "outbreak." As if the sentiments of humanity were ever found unaccompanied by its deeds, and you could disperse them, all finished to order, the pure article, as easily as water with a watering pot, and so lay the dust. What is that that I hear cast overboard? The bodies of the dead that have found deliverance. That is the way we are "diffusing" humanity and its sentiments with it.

Prominent and influential editors, accustomed to deal with politicians, men of an infinitely lower grade, say, in their ignorance, that he acted "on the principle of revenge." They do not know the man. They must enlarge themselves to conceive of him. I have no doubt that the time will come when they will begin to see him as he was. They have got to conceive of a man of faith and of religious principle, and not a politician nor an Indian; of a man who did not wait till he was personally interfered with or thwarted in some harmless business before he gave his life to the cause of the oppressed.

If Walker may be considered the representative of the South, I wish I could say that Brown was the representative of the North. He was a superior man. He did not value his bodily life in comparison with ideal things. He did not recognize unjust human laws but resisted them as he was bid. For once we are lifted out of the trivialness and dust of politics into the region of truth and manhood. No man in America has ever stood up so persistently and effectively for the dignity of human nature, knowing himself for a man and the equal of any and all governments. In that sense he was the most American of us all.

He needed no babbling lawyer, making false issues, to defend him. He was more than a match for all the judges that American voters, or office holders of whatever grade, can create. He could not have been tried by a jury of his peers, because his peers did not exist. When a man stands up serenely against the condemnation and vengeance of mankind, rising above them literally *by a whole body*—even though he were of late the vilest murderer who has settled that matter with himself—the spectacle is a sublime one—didn't ye know it, ye Liberators, ye Tribunes, ye Republicans? and we become criminal in comparison. Do yourselves the honor to recognize him. He needs none of your respect.

As for the Democratic journals, they are not human enough to affect me at all. I do not feel indignation at anything they may say.

I am aware that I anticipate a little, that he was still, at the last accounts, alive in the hands of his foes; but that being the case, I have all along found myself thinking and speaking of him as physically dead.

I do not believe in erecting statues to those who still live in our hearts, whose bones have not yet crumbled in the earth around us, but I would rather see the statue of Captain Brown in the Massachusetts Statehouse yard than that of any other man whom I know. I rejoice that I live in this age—that I am his contemporary.

What a contrast, when we turn to that political party which is so anxiously shuffling him and his plot out of its way and looking around for some available slaveholder, perhaps, to be its candidate, at least for one who will execute the Fugitive Slave Law, and all those other unjust laws which he took up arms to annul!

Insane! A father and six sons, and one son-in-law, and several more men besides—as many, at least, as twelve disciples—all struck with insanity at once; while the same tyrant holds with a firmer grip than ever his 4 million slaves, and a thousand sane editors, his abettors, are saving their country and their bacon! Just as insane were his efforts in Kansas. Ask the tyrant who is his most dangerous foe, the sane man or the insane. Do the thousands who know him best, who have rejoiced at his deeds in Kansas, and have afforded him material aid there, think him insane? Such a use of this word is a mere trope with most who persist in using it, and I have no doubt that many of the rest have already in silence retracted their words.

Read his admirable answers to Mason and others. How they are dwarfed and defeated by the contrast! On the one side, half-brutish, half-timid questioning; on the other, truth, clear as lightning, crashing into their obscene temples. They are made to stand with Pilate, and Gesler, and the Inquisition. How ineffectual their speech and action! And what a void their silence! They are but helpless tools in this great work. It was no human power that gathered them about this preacher.

What have Massachusetts and the North sent a few *sane* representatives to Congress for, of late years? to declare with effect what kind of sentiments? All their speeches put together and boiled down—and probably they themselves will confess it—do not match for manly directness and force, and for simple truth, the few casual remarks of crazy John Brown, on the floor of the Harpers Ferry engine house—that man whom you are about to hang, to send to the other world, though not to represent *you* there.

No, he was not our representative in any sense. He was too fair a specimen of a man to represent the like of us. Who, then, *were* his constituents? If you read his words understandingly, you will find out. In his case there is no idle eloquence, no made nor maiden speech, no compliments to the oppressor. Truth is his inspirer and earnestness the polisher of his sentences. He could afford to lose his Sharps rifles, while her retained his faculty of speech, a Sharps rifle of infinitely surer and longer range. ...

We talk about a *representative* government; but what a monster of a government is that where the noblest faculties of the mind, and the *whole* heart, are not *represented*. A semi-human tiger or ox, stalking over the earth, with its heart taken out and the top of its brain shot away. Heroes have fought well on their stumps when their legs were shot off, but I never heard of any good done by such a government as that.

The only government that I recognize—and it matters not how few are at the head of it or how small its army—is that power that establishes justice in the land, never that which establishes injustice. What shall we think of a government to which all the truly brave and just men in the land are enemies, standing between it and those whom it oppresses? A government that pretends to be Christian and crucifies a million Christs every day!

Treason! Where does such treason take its rise? I cannot help thinking of you as you deserve, ye governments. Can you dry up the fountains of thought? High treason, when it is resistance to tyranny here below, has its origin in, and is first committed by, the power that makes and forever recreates man. When you have caught and hung all these human rebels, you have accomplished nothing but your own guilt, for you have not struck at the fountainhead. You presume to contend with a foe against whom West Point cadets and rifled cannon *point* not. Can all the art of the cannon founder tempt matter to turn against its maker? Is the form in which the founder thinks he casts it more essential than the constitution of it and of himself?

The United States have a coffle of 4 million slaves. They are determined to keep them in this condition; and Massachusetts is one of the confederated overseers to prevent their escape. Such are not all the inhabitants of Massachusetts, but such are they who rule and are obeyed here. It was Massachusetts, as well as Virginia, that put down this insurrection at Harpers Ferry. She sent the Marines there, and she will have to pay the penalty of her sin. ...

It was [Brown's] peculiar doctrine that a man has a perfect right to interfere by force with the slaveholder in order to rescue the slave. I agree with him. They who are continually shocked by slavery have some right to be shocked by the violent death of the slaveholder, but no others. Such will be more shocked by his life than by his death. I shall not be forward to think him mistaken in his method who quickest succeeds to liberate the slave. I speak for the slave when I say that I prefer the philanthropy of Captain Brown to that philanthropy which neither shoots me nor liberates me. At any rate, I do not think it is quite sane for one to spend his whole life in talking or writing about this matter, unless he is continuously inspired, and I have not done so. A man may have other affairs to attend to. I do not wish to kill nor to be killed, but I can foresee circumstances in which both these things would be by me unavoidable.

We preserve the so-called peace of our community by deeds of petty violence every day. Look at the policemen's billy and handcuffs! Look at the jail! Look at the gallows! Look at the chaplain of the regiment! We are hoping only to live safely on the outskirts of *this* provisional army. So we defend ourselves and our hen roosts and maintain slavery. I know that the mass of my countrymen think that the only righteous use that can be made of Sharps rifles and revolvers is to fight duels with them when we are insulted by other nations, or to hunt Indians, or shoot fugitive slaves with them, or the like. I think that for once the Sharps rifles and the revolvers were employed in a righteous cause. The tools were in the hands of one who could use them.

The same indignation that is said to have cleared the temple once will clear it again. The question is not about the weapon but the spirit in which you use it. No man has appeared in America, as yet, who loved his fellowman so well and treated him so tenderly. He lived for him. He took up his life and he laid it down for him. What sort of violence is that which is encouraged, not by soldiers but by peaceable citizens, not so much by laymen as by ministers of the gospel, not so much by the fighting sects as by the Quakers, and not so much by Quaker men as by Quaker women? ...

Who is it whose safety requires that Captain Brown be hung? Is it indispensable to any Northern man? Is there no resource but to cast these men also to the Minotaur? If you do not wish it, say so distinctly. While these things are being done, beauty stands veiled and music is a screeching lie. Think of him—of his rare qualities! Such a man as it takes ages to make and ages to understand; no mock hero, nor the representative of any party. A man such as the sun may not rise upon again in this benighted land. To whose making went the costliest material, the finest adamant; sent to be the redeemer of those in captivity; and the only use to which you can put him is to hang him at the end of a rope! You who pretend to care for Christ crucified, consider what you are about to do to him who offered himself to be the savior of 4 million men. ...

I am here to plead his cause with you. I plead not for his life but for his character—his immortal life; and so it becomes your cause wholly and is not his in the least. Some 1,800 years ago, Christ was crucified; this morning, perchance, Captain Brown was hung. These are the two ends of a chain which is not without its links. He is not Old Brown any longer; he is an angel of light.

I see now that it was necessary that the bravest and humanest man in all the country should be hung. Perhaps he saw it himself. I *almost fear* that I may yet hear of his deliverance, doubting if a prolonged life, if *any* life, can do as much good as his death.

HENRY TIMROD:
ETHNOGENESIS (1861)

Source: *Poems*, Memorial Edition, Richmond, Va., 1901.

ETHNOGENESIS

I
Hath not the morning dawned with added light?
And shall not evening call another star

Out of the infinite regions of the night,
To mark this day in Heaven? At last, we are
A nation among nations; and the world
Shall soon behold in many a distant port
Another flag unfurled!
Now, come what may, whose favor need we court?
And, under God, whose thunder need we fear?
Thank Him who placed us here
Beneath so kind a sky—the very sun
Takes part with us; and on our errands run
All breezes of the ocean; dew and rain
Do noiseless battle for us; and the year,
And all the gentle daughters in her train,
March in our ranks, and in our service wield
Long spears of golden grain!
A yellow blossom as her fairy shield,
June flings her azure banner to the wind,
While in the order of their birth
Her sisters pass, and many an ample field
Grows white beneath their steps, till now, behold,
Its endless sheets unfold
The snow of Southern summers! Let the earth
Rejoice! beneath those fleeces soft and warm

Our happy land shall sleep
In a repose as deep
As if we lay entrenched behind
Whole leagues of Russian ice and
Arctic storm!

II
And what if, mad with wrongs
themselves have wrought,
In their own treachery caught,
By their own fears made bold,
And leagued with him of old,
Who long since in the limits of
the North,
Set up his evil throne, and warred
with God —
What if, both mad and blinded in
their rage
Our foes should fling us down
their mortal gage,
And with a hostile step profane
our sod!
We shall not shrink, my brothers,
but go forth
To meet them, marshaled by the
Lord of Hosts,
And overshadowed by the mighty
ghosts
Of Moultrie and Eutaw—who shall foil
Auxiliars such as these? Nor
these alone,
But every stock and stone
Shall help us; but the very soil,
And all the generous wealth it
gives to toil,
And all for which we love our
noble land,
Shall fight beside, and through us;
sea and strand,

The heart of woman, and her hand,
Tree, fruit, and flower, and every
influence,
Gentle, or grave, or grand;
The winds in our defense
Shall seem to blow; to us the hills
shall lend
Their firmness and their calm;
And in our stiffened sinews we
shall blend
The strength of pine and palm!

III
Nor would we shun the
battleground,
Though weak as we are strong;
Call up the clashing elements
around,
And test the right and wrong!
On one side, creeds that dare to
teach
What Christ and Paul refrained
to preach;
Codes built upon a broken pledge,
And charity that whets a pon-
iard's edge;
Fair schemes that leave the neigh-
boring poor
To starve and shiver at the schem-
er's door,
While in the world's most liberal
ranks enrolled,
He turns some vast philanthropy
to gold;
Religion, taking every mortal form
But that a pure and Christian
faith makes warm,
Where not to vile fanatic passion
urged,

Or not in vague philosophies submerged,
Repulsive with all Pharisaic leaven,
And making laws to stay the laws of Heaven!
And on the other, scorn of sordid gain,
Unblemished honor, truth without a stain,
Faith, justice, reverence, charitable wealth,
And, for the poor and humble, laws which give,
Not the mean right to buy the right to live,
But life, and home, and health!
To doubt the end were want of trust in God,
Who, if He has decreed
That we must pass a redder sea
Than that which rang to Miriam's holy glee,
Will surely raise at need
A Moses with his rod!

IV
But let our fears — if fears we have — be still,
And turn us to the future! Could we climb
Some mighty Alp, and view the coming time,
The rapturous sight would fill
Our eyes with happy tears!
Not only for the glories which the years
Shall bring us; not for lands from sea to sea,

And wealth, and power, and peace, though these shall be;
But for the distant peoples we shall bless,
And the hushed murmurs of a world's distress:
For, to give labor to the poor,
The whole sad planet o'er,
And save from want and crime the humblest door,
Is one among the many ends for which
God makes us great and rich!
The hour perchance is not yet wholly ripe
When all shall own it, but the type
Whereby we shall be known in every land
Is that vast gulf which lips our Southern strand,
And through the cold, untempered ocean pours
Its genial streams, that far off Arctic shores,
May sometimes catch upon the softened breeze
Strange tropic warmth and hints of summer seas.

ABRAHAM LINCOLN: FIRST INAUGURAL ADDRESS (1861)

Source: *A Compilation of the Messages and Papers of the Presidents 1789-1897*, James D. Richardson, ed., Washington, 1896–1899, Vol. VI, pp. 5–12.

In compliance with a custom as old as the government itself, I appear before you to address you briefly and to take, in your presence, the oath prescribed by the Constitution of the United States to be taken by the President "before he enters on the execution of his office."

I do not consider it necessary, at present, for me to discuss those matters of administration about which there is no special anxiety or excitement. Apprehension seems to exist among the people of the Southern states that, by the accession of a Republican administration, their property and their peace and personal security are to be endangered. There has never been any reasonable cause for such apprehension. Indeed, the most ample evidence to the contrary has all the while existed and been open to their inspection. It is found in nearly all the published speeches of him who now addresses you.

I do but quote from one of those speeches when I declare that "I have no purpose, directly or indirectly, to interfere with the institution of slavery in the states where it exists. I believe I have no lawful right to do so, and I have no inclination to do so." Those who nominated and elected me did so with full knowledge that I had made this and many similar declarations, and had never recanted them. And, more than this, they placed in the platform, for my acceptance; and as a law to themselves and to me, the clear and emphatic resolution which I now read:

> Resolved, *that the maintenance inviolate of the rights of the states, and especially the right of each state, to order and control its own*

> *domestic institutions according to its own judgment exclusively is essential to that balance of power on which the perfection and endurance of our political fabric depend; and we denounce the lawless invasion by armed force of the soil of any state or territory, no matter under what pretext, as among the gravest of crimes.*

I now reiterate these sentiments; and, in doing so, I only press upon the public attention the most conclusive evidence, of which the case is susceptible, that the property, peace, and security of no section are to be in any way endangered by the now incoming administration. I add, too, that all the protection which, consistently with the Constitution and the laws, can be given will be cheerfully given to all the states when lawfully demanded, for whatever cause—as cheerfully to one section as to another.

There is much controversy about the delivering up of fugitives from service or labor. The clause I now read is as plainly written in the Constitution as any other of its provisions:

> *No person held to service or labor in one state, under the laws thereof, escaping into another, shall, in consequence of any law or regulation therein, be discharged from such service or labor, but shall be delivered up on claim of the party to whom such service or labor may be due.*

It is scarcely questioned that this provision was intended by those who made it for the reclaiming of what we call fugitive slaves; and the intention of the lawgiver is the law.

All members of Congress swear their support to the whole Constitution—to this provision as much as to any other. To the proposition, then, that slaves whose cases come within the terms of this clause "shall be delivered up," their oaths are unanimous. Now, if they would make the effort in good temper, could they not, with nearly equal unanimity, frame and pass a law by means of which to keep good that unanimous oath?

There is some difference of opinion whether this clause should be enforced by national or by the state authority; but surely that difference is not a very material one. If the slave is to be surrendered, it can be of but little consequence to him or to others by which authority it is done. And should anyone, in any case, be content that his oath shall go unkept on a merely unsubstantial controversy as to *how* it shall be kept?

Again, in any law upon this subject, ought not all the safeguards of liberty known in civilized and humane jurisprudence to be introduced, so that a freeman be not, in any case, surrendered as a slave? And might it not be well, at the same time, to provide by law for the enforcement of that clause in the Constitution which guarantees that "the citizen of each state shall be entitled to all privileges and immunities of citizens in the several states"?

I take the official oath today with no mental reservations and with no purpose to construe the Constitution or laws by any hypercritical rules. And while I do not choose now to specify particular acts of Congress as proper to be enforced, I do suggest that it will be much safer for all, both in official and private stations, to conform to and abide by all those acts which stand unrepealed than to violate any of them, trusting to find impunity in having them held to be unconstitutional.

It is seventy-two years since the first inauguration of a President under our national Constitution. During that period fifteen different and greatly distinguished citizens have, in succession, administered the executive branch of the government. They have conducted it through many perils, and generally with great success. Yet, with all this scope of precedent, I now enter upon the same task for the brief constitutional term of four years under great and peculiar difficulties.

A disruption of the federal Union, heretofore only menaced, is now formidably attempted.

I hold that, in contemplation of universal law and of the Constitution, the Union of these states is perpetual. Perpetuity is implied, if not expressed, in the fundamental law of all national governments. It is safe to assert that no government proper ever had a provision in its organic law for its own termination. Continue to execute all the express provisions of our national Constitution, and the Union will endure forever—it being impossible to destroy it except by some action not provided for in the instrument itself.

Again, if the United States be not a government proper, but an association of states in the nature of contract merely, can it, as a contract, be peaceably unmade by less than all the parties who made it? One party to a contract may violate it—break it, so to speak—but does it not require all to lawfully rescind it? Descending from these general principles, we find the proposition that in legal contemplation, the Union is perpetual, confirmed by the history of the Union itself.

The Union is much older than the Constitution. It was formed, in fact, by the Articles of Association in 1774. It was matured and continued by the Declaration of Independence in 1776. It was further matured, and the faith of all the then thirteen states expressedly plighted and engaged, that it should be perpetual by the Articles of Confederation of 1778. And finally, in 1787, one of the declared objects for ordaining and establishing the Constitution, was *"to form a more perfect Union."*

But if destruction of the Union by one or by a part only of the states be lawfully possible, the Union is *less* perfect than before the Constitution, having lost the vital element of perpetuity.

It follows from these views that no state, upon its own mere motion, can lawfully get out of the Union—that *resolves* and *ordinances* to that effect are legally void; and that acts of violence within any state or states against the authority of the United States are insurrectionary or revolutionary, according to circumstances.

I therefore consider that, in view of the Constitution and the laws, the Union is unbroken; and to the extent of my ability, I shall take care, as the Constitution itself expressly enjoins upon me, that the laws of the Union be faithfully executed in all the states. Doing this I deem to be only a simple duty on my part; and I shall perform it, so far as practicable, unless my rightful masters, the American people, shall withhold the requisite means or in some authoritative manner direct the contrary.

I trust this will not be regarded as a menace but only as the declared purpose of the Union that it *will* constitutionally defend and maintain itself. In doing this, there needs to be no bloodshed or violence; and there shall be none unless it be forced upon the national authority.

The power confided to me will be used to hold, occupy, and possess the property and places belonging to the government, and to collect the duties and imposts; but beyond what may be necessary for these objects, there will be no invasion—no using of force against or among the people anywhere.

Where hostility to the United States, in any interior locality, shall be so great and universal as to prevent competent resident citizens from holding the federal offices, there will be no attempt to force obnoxious strangers among the people for that object. While the strict legal right may exist in the government to enforce the exercise of these offices, the attempt to do so would be so irritating, and so nearly impracticable withal, that I deem it best to forego, for the time, the uses of such offices.

The mails, unless repelled, will continue to be furnished in all parts of the Union.

So far as possible, the people everywhere shall have that sense of perfect security which is most favorable to calm thought and reflection.

The course here indicated will be followed unless current events and experience shall show a modification or change to be proper; and in every case and exigency, my best discretion will be exercised, according to circumstances actually existing, and with a view and a hope of a peaceful solution of the national troubles, and the restoration of fraternal sympathies and affections.

That there are persons in one section or another who seek to destroy the Union at all events and are glad of any pretext to do it, I will neither affirm or deny; but if there be such, I need address no word to them. To those, however, who really love the Union, may I not speak?

Before entering upon so grave a matter as the destruction of our national fabric, with all its benefits, its memories, and its hopes, would it not be wise to ascertain precisely why we do it? Will you hazard so desperate a step while there is any possibility that any portion of the ills you fly from have no real existence? Will you, while the certain ills you fly to are greater than all the real ones you fly from—will you risk the commission of so fearful a mistake?

All profess to be content in the Union if all constitutional rights can be maintained. Is it true, then, that any right plainly written in the Constitution has been denied? I think not. Happily, the human mind is so constituted that no party can reach to the audacity of doing this. Think, if you can, of a single instance in which a plainly written provision of the Constitution has ever been denied. If, by the mere force of numbers, a majority should deprive a minority of any clearly written constitutional right, it might, in a moral point of view, justify revolution—certainly would, if such right were a vital one. But such is not our case.

All the vital rights of minorities and of individuals are so plainly assured to them by affirmations and negations, guarantees and prohibitions, in the Constitution that controversies never arise concerning them. But no organic law can ever be framed with a provision specifically applicable to every question which may occur in practical administration. No foresight can anticipate nor any document of reasonable length contain express provisions for all possible questions. Shall fugitives from labor be surrendered by national or by state authority? The Constitution does not expressly say. *May* Congress prohibit slavery in the territories? The Constitution does not expressly say. *Must* Congress protect slavery in the territories? The Constitution does not expressly say.

From questions of this class spring all our constitutional controversies, and we divide upon them into majorities and minorities. If the minority will not acquiesce, the majority must, or the government must cease. There is no other alternative; for continuing the government is acquiescence on one side or the other. If a minority, in such case, will secede rather than acquiesce, they make a precedent which in turn will divide and ruin them; for a minority of their own will secede from them whenever a majority refuses to be controlled by such minority.

For instance, why may not any portion of a new confederacy, a year or two hence, arbitrarily secede again, precisely as portions of the present Union now claim to secede from it? All who cherish disunion sentiments are now being educated to the exact temper of doing this. Is there such perfect identity of interests among the states to compose a new Union as to produce harmony only and prevent renewed secession?

Plainly, the central idea of secession is the essence of anarchy. A majority, held in restraint by constitutional checks and limitations, and always changing easily with deliberate changes of popular opinions and sentiments, is the only true sovereign of a free people. Whoever rejects it does of necessity fly to anarchy or to despotism. Unanimity is impossible. The rule of a minority, as a permanent arrangement, is wholly inadmissible; so that, rejecting the majority principle, anarchy or despotism in some form is all that is left.

I do not forget the position assumed by some, that constitutional questions are to be decided by the Supreme Court; nor do I deny that such decisions must be binding in any case upon the parties to a suit as to the object of that suit, while they are also entitled to very high respect and consideration, in all parallel cases, by all other departments of the government. And while it is obviously possible that such decision may be erroneous in any given case, still the evil effect following it, being limited to that particular case, with the chance that it may be overruled and never become a precedent for other cases, can better be borne than could the evils of a different practice.

At the same time, the candid citizen must confess that if the policy of the government, upon vital questions affecting the whole people, is to be irrevocably fixed by decisions of the Supreme Court, the instant they are made, in ordinary litigation between parties in personal actions, the people will have ceased to be their own rulers, having, to that extent, practically resigned their government into the hands of that eminent tribunal.

Nor is there, in this view, any assault upon the Court or the judges. It is a duty from which they may not shrink to decide cases properly brought before them; and it is no fault of theirs if others seek to turn their decisions to political purposes.

One section of our country believes slavery is *right* and ought to be extended, while the other believes it is *wrong* and ought not to be extended. This is the only substantial dispute. The fugitive slave clause of the Constitution and the law for the suppression of the foreign slave trade are each as well enforced, perhaps, as any law can ever be in a community where the moral sense of the people imperfectly supports the law itself. The great body of the people abide by the dry legal obligation in both cases, and a few break over in each. This, I think, cannot be perfectly cured; and it would be worse in both cases *after* the separation of the sections than before. The foreign slave trade, now imperfectly suppressed, would be ultimately revived without restriction in one section; while fugitive slaves, now only partially surrendered, would not be surrendered at all by the other.

Physically speaking, we cannot separate. We cannot remove our respective sections from each other, nor build an impassable wall between them. A husband and wife may be divorced, and go out of the presence and beyond the reach of each other; but the different parts of our country cannot do this. They cannot but remain face to face; and intercourse, either amicable or hostile, must continue between them. Is it possible, then, to make that intercourse more advantageous or more satisfactory *after* separation than *before?* Can aliens make treaties easier than friends can make laws? Can treaties be more faithfully enforced between aliens than laws can among friends? Suppose you go to war, you cannot fight always; and when, after much loss on both sides and no gain on either, you cease fighting, the identical old questions as to terms of intercourse are again upon you.

This country, with its institutions, belongs to the people who inhabit it. Whenever they shall grow weary of the existing government, they can exercise their *constitutional* right of amending it or their *revolutionary* right to dismember or overthrow it. I cannot be ignorant of the fact that many worthy and patriotic citizens are desirous of having the national Constitution amended. While I make no recommendation of amendments, I fully recognize the rightful authority of the people over the whole subject, to be exercised in either of the modes prescribed in the instrument itself; and I should, under existing circumstances, favor rather than oppose a fair opportunity being afforded the people to act upon it.

I will venture to add that, to me, the convention mode seems preferable, in that it allows amendments to originate with the people themselves, instead of only permitting them to take or reject propositions originated by others, not especially chosen for the purpose, and which might not be precisely such as they would wish to either accept or refuse. I understand a proposed amendment to the Constitution—which amendment, however, I have not seen— has passed Congress, to the effect that the federal government shall never interfere with the domestic institutions of the states, including that of persons held to service. To avoid misconstruction of what I have said, I depart from my purpose not to speak of particular amendments so far as to say that, holding such a provision to now be implied constitutional law, I have no objection to its being made express and irrevocable.

The chief magistrate derives all his authority from the people, and they have conferred none upon him to fix terms for the separation of the states. The people themselves can do this also if they choose; but the executive, as such, has nothing to do with it. His duty is to administer the present government, as it came to his hands, and to transmit it, unimpaired by him, to his successor. Why should there not be a patient confidence in the ultimate justice of the people? Is there any better or equal hope in the world? In our present differences, is either party without faith of being in the right?

If the Almighty Ruler of nations, with His eternal truth and justice, be on your side of the North, or on yours of the South, that truth and that justice will surely prevail, by the judgment of this great tribunal, the American people. By the frame of the government under which we live, this same people have wisely given their public servants but little power for mischief; and have, with equal wisdom, provided for the return of that little to their own hands at very short intervals. While the people retain their virtue and vigilance, no administration, by any extreme of wickedness or folly, can very seriously injure the government in the short space of four years.

My countrymen, one and all, think calmly and *well* upon this whole subject. Nothing valuable can be lost by taking time. If there be an object to *hurry* any of you, in hot haste, to a step which you would never take *deliberately*, that object will be frustrated by taking time; but no good object can be frustrated by it.

Such of you as are now dissatisfied still have the old Constitution unimpaired, and, on the sensitive point, the laws of your own framing under it; while the new administration will have no immediate power, if it would, to change either.

If it were admitted that you who are dissatisfied hold the right side in the dispute, there still is no single good reason for precipitate action. Intelligence, patriotism, Christianity, and a firm reliance on Him, who has never yet forsaken this favored land, are still competent to adjust, in the best way, all our present difficulty.

In *your* hands, my dissatisfied fellow countrymen, and not in *mine* is the momentous issue of civil war. The government will not assail *you*. You can have no conflict without being yourselves the aggressors. *You* have no oath registered in heaven to destroy the government, while *I* shall have the most solemn one to "preserve, protect, and defend" it.

I am loathe to close. We are not enemies but friends. We must not be enemies. Though passion may have strained, it must not break our bonds of affection.

The mystic chords of memory, stretching from every battlefield and patriot grave to every living heart and hearthstone all over this broad land, will yet swell the chorus of the Union, when again touched, as surely they will be, by the better angels of our nature.

JOHN S. ROCK: AFRICAN AMERICAN HOPES FOR EMANCIPATION (1862)

Source: *Liberator*, Feb. 14, 1862.

Ladies and Gentlemen:

I am here not so much to make a speech as to add a little more *color* to this occasion.

I do not know that it is right that I should speak at this time, for it is said that we have talked too much already; and it is being continually thundered in our ears that the time for speechmaking has ended, and the time for action has arrived. Perhaps this is so. This may be the theory of the people, but we all know that the *active* idea has found but little sympathy with either of our great military commanders or the national executive; for they have told us, again and again, that "patience is a cure for all sores," and that we must wait for the "good time," which, to us, has been long a-coming.

It is not my desire, neither is it the time for me, to criticize the government, even if I had the disposition so to do. The situation of the black man in this country is far from being an enviable one. Today, our heads are in the lion's mouth, and we must get them out the best way we can. To contend against the government is as difficult as it is to sit in Rome and fight with the pope. It is probable that, if we had the malice of the Anglo-Saxon, we would watch our chances and seize the first opportunity to take our revenge. If we attempted this, the odds would be against us, and the first thing we should know would be—*nothing!* The most of us are capable of perceiving that the man who spits against the wind spits in his own face!

While Mr. Lincoln has been more conservative than I had hoped to find him, I recognize in him an honest man, striving to redeem the country from the degradation and shame into which Mr. Buchanan and his predecessors have plunged it.

This nation is mad. In its devoted attachment to the Negro, it has run crazy after him; and now, having caught him, hangs on with a deadly grasp, and says to him, with more earnestness and pathos than Ruth expressed to Naomi, "Where thou goest, I will go; where thou lodgest, I will lodge; thy people shall be my people, and thy God my God." ...

I do not deny that there is a deep and cruel prejudice lurking in the bosoms of the white people of this country. It is much more abundant in the North than in the South. Here, it is to be found chiefly among the higher and lower classes; and there is no scarcity of it among the poor whites at the South.

The cause of this prejudice may be seen at a glance. The educated and wealthy class despise the Negro because they have robbed him of his hard earnings or, at least, have got rich off the fruits of his labor; and they believe if he gets his freedom, their fountain will be dried up, and they will be obliged to seek business in a new channel. Their "occupation will be gone." The lowest class hate him because he is poor, as they are, and is a competitor with them for the same labor. The poor, ignorant white man, who does not understand that the interest of the laboring classes is mutual, argues in this wise: "Here is so much labor to be performed, that darkey does it. If he was gone, I should have his place." The rich and the poor are both prejudiced from interest, and not because they entertain vague notions of justice and humanity.

While uttering my solemn protest against this American vice, which has done more than any other thing to degrade the American people in the eyes of the civilized world, I am happy to state that there are many who have never known this sin, and many others who have been converted to the truth by the "foolishness of antislavery preaching," and are deeply interested in the welfare of the race, and never hesitate to use their means and their influence to help break off the yoke that has been so long crushing us. I thank them all and hope the number may be multiplied, until we shall have a people who will know no man save by his virtues and his merits.

Now, it seems to me that a blind man can see that the present war is an effort to nationalize, perpetuate, and extend slavery in this country. In short, slavery is the cause of the war: I might say, is *the* war itself. Had it not been for slavery, we should have had no war! Through 240 years of indescribable tortures, slavery has wrung out of the blood, bones, and muscles of the Negro hundreds of millions of dollars and helped much to make this nation rich. At the same time, it has developed a volcano which has burst forth, and, in a less number of days than years, has dissipated this wealth and rendered the government bankrupt! And, strange as it may appear, you still cling to this monstrous iniquity, notwithstanding it is daily sinking the country lower and lower! Some of our ablest and best men have been sacrificed to appease the wrath of this American god. ...

The government wishes to bring back the country to what it was before. This is possible; but what is to be gained by it? If we are fools enough to retain the cancer that is eating out our vitals, when we can safely extirpate it, who will pity us if we see our mistake when we are past recovery? The Abolitionists saw this day of tribulation and reign of terror long ago, and warned you of it; *but you would not hear!* You now say that it is their agitation which has brought about this terrible civil war! That is to say, your friend sees a slow match set near a keg of gunpowder in your house and timely warns you of the danger which he sees is inevitable; you despise his warning, and, after the explosion, say, if he had not told you of it, it would not have happened!

Now, when some leading men who hold with the policy of the President, and yet pretend to be liberal, argue that while they are willing to admit that the slave has an undoubted right to his liberty, the master has an equal right to his property; that to liberate the slave would be to injure the master, and a greater good would be accomplished to the country in these times by the loyal master's retaining his property than by giving to the slave his liberty—I do not understand it so. Slavery is treason against God, man, and the nation. The master has no right to be a partner in a conspiracy which has shaken the very foundation of the government. Even to apologize for it, while in open rebellion, is to aid and abet in treason. The master's right to his property in human flesh cannot be equal to the slave's right to his liberty.

The former right is acquired, either by kidnaping or unlawful purchase from kidnapers, or inheritance from kidnapers. The very claim invalidates itself. On the other hand, liberty is the inalienable right of every human being; and liberty can make no compromise with slavery. ...

Today, when it is a military necessity, and when the safety of the country is dependent upon emancipation, our humane political philosophers are puzzled to know what would become of the slaves if they were emancipated! The idea seems to prevail that the poor things would suffer if robbed of the glorious privileges that they now enjoy! If they could not be flogged, half starved, and work to support in ease and luxury those who have never waived an opportunity to outrage and wrong them, they would pine away and die! Do you imagine that the Negro can live outside of slavery? Of course, now, they can take care of themselves and their masters too; but if you give them their liberty, must they not suffer?

Have you never been able to see through all this? Have you not observed that the location of this organ of sympathy is in the pocket of the slaveholder and the man who shares in the profits of slave labor? Of course you have; and pity those men who have lived upon their ill-gotten wealth. You know, if they do not have somebody to work for them, they must leave their gilded *salons*, and take off their coats and roll up their sleeves, and take their chances among the *live* men of the world. This, you are aware, these respectable gentlemen will not do, for they have been so long accustomed to live by robbing and cheating the Negro that they are sworn never to work while they can live by plunder.

Can the slaves take care of themselves? What do you suppose becomes of the thousands who fly, ragged and penniless, from the South every year, and scatter themselves throughout the free states of the North? Do they take care of themselves? I am neither ashamed nor afraid to meet this question. Assertions like this, long uncontradicted, seem to be admitted as established facts. I ask your attention for one moment to the fact that colored men at the North are shut out of almost every avenue to wealth, and, yet, strange to say, the proportion of paupers is much less among us than among you!

Are the beggars in the streets of Boston colored men? In Philadelphia, where there is a larger free colored population than is to be found in any other city in the free states, and where we are denied every social privilege, and are not even permitted to send our children to the schools that we are taxed to support, or to ride in the city horsecars, yet even there we pay taxes enough to support our own poor, and have a balance of a few thousand in our favor, which goes to support those "poor whites" who "can't take care of themselves."

Many of those who advocate emancipation as a military necessity seem puzzled to know what is best to be done with the slave if he is set at liberty. Colonization in Africa, Haiti, Florida, and South America are favorite theories with many well-informed persons. This is really interesting! No wonder Europe does not sympathize with you. You are the only people, claiming to be civilized, who take away the rights of those whose color differs from your own. If you find that you cannot rob the Negro of his labor and of himself, you will banish him! What a sublime idea! You are certainly a great people! What is your plea? Why, that the slaveholders will not permit us to live among them as freemen, and that the air of northern latitudes is not good for us! Let me tell you, my friends, *the slaveholders are not the men we dread!* They do not desire to have us removed. The Northern pro-slavery men have done the free people of color tenfold more injury than the Southern slaveholders. In the South, it is simply a question of dollars and cents. The slaveholder cares no more for you than he does for me. They enslave their own children and sell them, and they would as soon enslave white men as black men.

The secret of the slaveholder's attachment to slavery is to be found in the dollar, and *that* he is determined to get without working for it. There is no prejudice against color among the slaveholders. Their social system and 1 million mulattoes are facts which no arguments can demolish. If the slaves were emancipated, they would remain where they are. Black labor in the South is at a premium. The freeman of color there has always had the preference over the white laborer. Many of you are aware that Southerners will do a favor for a free colored man when they will not do it for a white man in the same condition in life. They believe in their institution because it supports them. ...

Other countries are held out as homes for us. Why is this? Why is it that the people from all other countries are invited to come here, and we are asked to go away? Is it to make room for the refuse population of Europe? ... Does anyone pretend to deny that this is our country, or that much of the wealth and prosperity found here is the result of the labor of our hands? ... The free people of color have succeeded, in spite of every effort to crush them, and we are today a living refutation of that shameless assertion that we "can't take care of ourselves" in a state of freedom. ...

When the orange is squeezed, we throw it aside. The black man is a good fellow while he is a slave and toils for nothing; but the moment he claims his own flesh and blood and bones, he is a most obnoxious creature, and there is a proposition to get rid of him! He is happy while he remains a poor, degraded, ignorant slave, without even the right to his own offspring. While in this condition, the master can ride in the same carriage, sleep in the same bed, and nurse from the same bosom. But give this same slave the right to use his own legs, his hands, his body, and his mind, and this happy and desirable creature is instantly transformed into a miserable and loathsome wretch, fit only to be colonized somewhere near the mountains of the moon or eternally banished from the presence of all civilized beings. You must not lose sight of the fact that it is the emancipated slave and the free colored man whom it is proposed to remove—not the slave. This country and climate are perfectly adapted to Negro slavery; it is the free black that the air is not good for! What an idea! A country good for slavery and not good for freedom! ... *All the emigration and colonization societies that have been formed have been auxiliaries of the Slave Power and established for this purpose and the grand desire to make money out of our necessities. ...*

I do not regard this trying hour as a dark one. The war that has been waged on us for more than two centuries has opened our eyes and caused us to form alliances, so that instead of acting on the defensive, we are now prepared to attack the enemy. This is simply a change of tactics. I think I see the finger of God in all this. Yes, *there* is the handwriting on the wall: *I come not to bring peace, but the sword. Break every yoke, and let the oppressed go free. I have heard the groans of my people and am come down to deliver them! ...*

This rebellion for slavery means something! Out of it emancipation must spring. I do not agree with those men who see no hope in this war. There is nothing in it but hope. Our cause is onward. As it is with the sun, the clouds often obstruct his vision, but in the end we find there has been no standing still. It is true the government is but little more antislavery now than it was at the commencement of the war; but while fighting for its own existence, it has been obliged to take slavery by the throat and, sooner or later, *must* choke her to death.

ABRAHAM LINCOLN: EMANCIPATION PROCLAMATION (1863)

Source: *The Public Statutes at Large of the United States of America*, Vol. XII, pp. 1,268–1,269.

Whereas, on the 22nd day of September, in the year of our Lord 1862, a proclamation was issued by the President of the United States, containing, among other things, the following, to wit:

That on the 1st day of January, in the year of our Lord 1863, all persons held as slaves within any state or designated part of a state, the people whereof shall then be in rebellion against the United States, shall be then, thenceforward, and forever free; and the executive government of the United States, including the military and naval authority thereof, will recognize and maintain the freedom of such persons and will do no act or acts to repress such persons, or any of them, in any efforts they may make for their actual freedom.

That the executive will, on the 1st day of January aforesaid, by proclamation, designate the states and parts of states, if any, in which the people thereof, respectively, shall then be in rebellion against the United States; and the fact that any state or the people thereof shall on that day be in good faith represented in the Congress of the United States by members chosen thereto at elections wherein a majority of the qualified voters of such states shall have participated shall, in the absence of strong countervailing testimony, be deemed conclusive evidence that such state and the people thereof are not then in rebellion against the United States.

Now, therefore, I, Abraham Lincoln, President of the United States, by virtue of the power in me vested as commander in chief of the Army and Navy of the United States, in time of actual armed rebellion against the authority and government of the United States, and as a fit and necessary war measure for suppressing said rebellion, do, on this 1st day of January, in the year of our Lord 1863, and in accordance with my purpose so to do, publicly proclaimed for the full period of 100 days from the day first above mentioned, order and designate as the states and parts of states wherein the people thereof, respectively, are this day in rebellion against the United States the following, to wit:

Arkansas, Texas, Louisiana (except the parishes of St. Bernard, Plaquemines, Jefferson, St. John, St. Charles, St.

James, Ascension, Assumption, Terrebonne, Lafourche, St. Mary, St. Martin, and Orleans, including the city of New Orleans), Mississippi, Alabama, Florida, Georgia, South Carolina, North Carolina, and Virginia (except the forty-eight counties designated as West Virginia, and also the counties of Berkeley, Accomac, Northampton, Elizabeth City, York, Princess Anne, and Norfolk, including the cities of Norfolk and Portsmouth), and which excepted parts are for the present left precisely as if this proclamation were not issued.

And, by virtue of the power and for the purpose aforesaid, I do order and declare that all persons held as slaves within said designated states and parts of states are, and henceforward shall be, free; and that the executive government of the United States, including the military and naval authorities thereof, will recognize and maintain the freedom of said persons.

And I hereby enjoin upon the people so declared to be free to abstain from all violence, unless in necessary self-defense; and I recommend to them that, in all cases when allowed, they labor faithfully for reasonable wages.

And I further declare and make known that such persons of suitable condition will be received into the armed service of the United States to garrison forts, positions, stations, and other places, and to man vessels of all sorts in said service.

And upon this act, sincerely believed to be an act of justice, warranted by the Constitution upon military necessity, I invoke the considerate judgment of mankind and the gracious favor of Almighty God.

CLEMENT L. VALLANDIGHAM: A PLEA TO STOP THE WAR (1863)

Source: *Speeches, Arguments, Addresses, and Letters of Clement L. Vallandigham,* New York, 1864, pp. 479–502.

The men who are in power at Washington, extending their agencies out through the cities and states of the Union and threatening to reinaugurate a reign of terror, may as well know that we comprehend precisely their purpose. I beg leave to assure you that it cannot and will not be permitted to succeed. The people of this country endorsed it once because they were told that it was essential to "the speedy suppression or crushing out of the rebellion" and the restoration of the Union; and they so loved the Union of these states that they would consent, even for a little while, under the false and now broken promises of the men in power, to surrender those liberties in order that the great object might, as was promised, be accomplished speedily.

They have been deceived; instead of crushing out the rebellion, the effort has been to crush out the spirit of liberty. The conspiracy of those in power is not so much for a vigorous prosecution of the war against rebels in the South as against the democracy in peace at home. ...

I am ready to submit to many things that I think had better not be attempted, just so long as assemblages of the people and the ballot, which are the great correctives of evil and which were intended by our fathers to be the machinery by which peaceable revolution should be accomplished in our government, remain untouched; but I say to the administration: "Lay not your hands at the foundation of the fabric of our liberties: you may lop off a branch here and there, and it will survive; we may tolerate that for the sake of a greater good hereafter; but whenever you reach forth your hand to strike at the very vitals of public liberty, then the people must and will determine in their sovereign capacity what remedy the occasion demands. ..."

Coming immediately from Washington, having witnessed, with the common satisfaction of the people of this country, the expiration of the Thirty-seventh Congress, I am here to speak, in the first place, briefly of some things which have been done in that body during the recent session and the session which preceded it. I will not go back so far as the extra session when general insanity prevailed throughout the country, and when the representatives of the people were, perhaps, to a larger degree excusable; because while they had doubtless contributed to that insanity, it was reflected back upon them again; but after a period given for meditation, after the logic of events had begun to work out, after the experiment of war had been tried for one year, it seems to me that wise men, men in whose hands you can with safety deposit the power that belongs to you, should have meditated a little while, and with some degree of wisdom have proceeded to legislate for the true interests of the country. Did they do it?

What has been the legislation financially, to begin with that? Where were we then? What was your currency? Gold. How much have you seen lately of it? You read of it in the stock market, impalpable, invisible—a thing that belongs to the past; it will go into the collections of those who have a curiosity for coins. What is your currency now? Greenbacks; nor is that all. Postage currency, and to what extent? Nearly a thousand millions already. That is what is offered to you. It is the entertainment to which you were invited, or rather which you were compelled to accept though not invited to, in 1860.

Your public debt—what was it then? The enormous sum of $71 million. Would you not be willing to compromise on that today? No doubt even they to whom that word "compromise" is most odious, who feel toward it as Romeo toward the word "banishment," would be very willing to settle the debt of this country at $71 million. It is now, actually or prospectively, because the appropriations reach that extent—$2,277,000,000.

That is the sum which this Congress has appropriated. They have given to this tremendous debt the power that belongs to it by the issuing of what is called a government currency, binding everybody by some sort of paper tie to the government—by the establishment of a grand national paper mill, a national bank, and through the other schemes of finance which were formed in the brain, or found a lodgment there somehow or other, of the secretary of the treasury. They have, by this instrumentality, obtained absolute control of the entire country. Through a tax law, the like of which never was imposed upon any but a conquered people, they have possession, actually or prospectively, of the entire property of the people of the country. Thus the purse, through the swift and anxious servility of a Congress which was intended by our fathers to be the watchful guardian of the people's money and the people's property, is now absolutely and unqualifiedly for two years at the disposal of the Executive of the United States.

In ordinary times, the control of that purse was regarded by the jealous lovers of liberty, by the men who preceded those in power, by the men who sat in your places twenty, thirty, or forty years ago, as one of the instruments of despotism—then even when our revenue was down as low as $20 million. It was then that, with jealousy, with the most scrutinizing care, every appropriation of money was allowed to pass through the House of Representatives or the Senate of the United States. And yet this Congress, since the 4th of July, 1861, some twenty months or less, has appropriated, as I have said, the enormous sum, and put it at the disposal of the President of the United States, of $2,277,000,000. And for what? To control that which in part is the lifeblood of the nation, its business, its currency, all that enter into the business transactions of life.

Part of it was intended in the beginning as a fund wherewith to set up the Negro trade. It entered the mind of Mr. Lincoln that the idea of compensated emancipation, as he calls it, must be carried out practically, and it found a place in his message and was repeated in the annual message, and that most delicate term to conceal a most odious thing—compensated emancipation—was given to it with the vain idea of deceiving the people—compensated emancipation meaning, being interpreted into good old-fashioned English—*Greenback Abolition.*

The minority in the Senate and in the House, through their pertinacity of purpose, surrounded though they were by bayonets and by despotic power on every side, succeeded at last in defeating this scheme for the purchase of Negroes; but nearly all the other plans were consummated. Thus, as I have said, the purse was placed under the control of the executive for two years. ...

And now, as to that other great weapon of government—the sword. ... Not only have ... 937,000 enlisted men and ... 300,000 drafted men—indeed, I might say ... 1,237,000 enlisted men, for the draft was used only to compel and procure enlistments—not only have all these men been sent into the field, or at least made to appear on the payrolls, but in the very expiring hours of the Congress, which died and went to its own

place at 12 o'clock on the 4th of March, your misrepresentatives—for such they had become—not speaking the voice of the people, did attempt to clothe the President with the power of conscripting every man in the United States between the ages of twenty and forty-five—to compel him to enter the Army and enable the President to keep up a war which, by that bill itself, he and they confess to be against the will of the people. ...

Thus, so far as it is possible, by an enactment having the form of law, the Congress of the United States have surrendered, absolutely, the entire military power of the country to the President. Now, if in possession of the purse and the sword absolutely and unqualifiedly, for two years, there be anything else wanting which describes a dictatorship, I beg to know what it is. Why did they not imitate the manhood of the old Roman senators when the exigency of the Republic, in their judgment, demanded it, and declare Mr. Lincoln a dictator in terms? That was alone absolutely what they meant—instead of, cowardlike, undertaking, in the form of law and by the abuse of constitutional power, to give the same authority and the same agencies to establish a despotism as would have been implied by the direct creation of a dictatorship. ...

As originally proposed, the bill not only would have but the 3 or 4 million males between twenty and forty-five under the military control of the President, as commander in chief, but would also have placed every man, woman, and child, by virtue of the two provisions that were stricken out, also in his power. Our civil rights would have been gone, and our judiciary undermined, and he would have been an absolute and uncontrolled dictator, with the power of Cincinnatus, but without one particle of his virtues.

Yet, unfortunately, while this much was accomplished on that bill, the same tyrannical power was conferred by another bill which passed both houses, and is now, so far as forms are concerned, a law of the land—at least an act of the Thirty-seventh Congress. It authorizes the President, whom the people made, whom the people had chosen by the ballot box under the Constitution and laws, to suspend the writ of habeas corpus all over the United States; to say that because there is a rebellion in South Carolina, a man shall not have freedom of speech, freedom of the press, or any of his rights untrammeled in the state of New York, or 1,000 miles distant. That was the very question upon which the people passed judgment in the recent elections, more, perhaps, than any other question. ...

The Constitution gives the power to Congress, and to Congress alone, to suspend the writ of habeas corpus, but it can only be done in case of invasion or rebellion, and then only when the public safety requires it; and in the opinion of the best jurists of the land, and indeed of everyone previous to these times, Congress could only suspend this writ in places actually in rebellion or actually invaded. That is the Constitution. And whenever this question shall be tried before a court in the state of New York, or Ohio, or Wisconsin, or anywhere else, before honest and fearless judges worthy of the place they occupy, the decision will be that it is unconstitutional, ...

The foreigner who seeks citizenship takes an express oath to support the Constitution of the United States. The man born under the tyranny of Austria or Russia—these used to be tyrannies before we had one of our own—that man born thus, with all his ideas formed upon the model of such governments, comes here; and yet it never entered into the heads of our fathers, from the beginning down to the present day, to require of him, through the naturalization laws, the taking of any other oath than to withdraw his allegiance to any foreign potentate and support the Constitution. But our own native-born citizens, and foreigners who have become citizens, who have taken that oath, are required, notwithstanding their innocence, to take this other oath. And though the informers, despicable as the vermin are, have failed to invent or devise any accusation whereby he can be held, he is required to take it; and if he refuse, he is then to remain imprisoned during the pleasure of the President of the United States. These are our liberties, forsooth!

Was it this which you were promised, in 1860, in that grand "Wide Awake" campaign, when banners were borne through your streets inscribed "Free speech, free press, and free men"? And all this has been accomplished, so far as the forms of the law go, by the Congress which has just expired. Now, I repeat again, that if there is anything wanting to make up a complete and absolute despotism, as iron and inexorable in its character as the worst despotisms of the Old World, or the most detestable of modern times, even to Bomba's of Naples, I am unable to comprehend what it is.

All this, gentlemen, infamous and execrable as it is, is enough to make the blood of the coldest man who has one single appreciation in his heart of freedom to boil with indignation. Still, so long as they leave to us free assemblages, free discussion, and a free ballot, I do not want to see, and will not encourage or countenance, any other mode of ridding ourselves of it.

We are ready to try these questions in that way; but I have only to repeat what I said a little while ago, that when the attempt is made to take away those other rights, and the only instrumentalities peaceably of reforming and correcting abuses—free assemblages, free speech, free ballot, and free elections—then the hour will have arrived when it will be the duty of freemen to find some other and efficient mode of defending their liberties.

Our fathers did not inaugurate the Revolution of 1776, they did not endure the sufferings and privations of a seven years' war to escape from the mild and moderate control of a constitutional monarchy like that of England, to be at last, in the third generation, subjected to a tyranny equal to that of any upon the face of the globe.

But, sir, I repeat, that it will not, in my judgment, come to this. I do not believe that this administration will undertake to deprive us of that right. I do not think it will venture, for one moment, to attempt to prevent, under any pretext whatever, the assembling together of the people for the fair discussion of their measures and policy. I do not believe it, because it seems to me with all the folly and madness which have been manifested in those high places, they must foresee what will inevitably follow. ...

In the beginning you were told that the purpose of all the power, previous to the recent legislation of Congress, given to or usurped by the executive, was for the maintenance of the Constitution and the restoration of the Union; and with that love for both, which is the highest honor to this people and its only apology (and it will be so recorded) for submitting to what we have done, the people made sacrifices, gave money, sent forth their firstborn at the call of the executive as no other people ever did since the world began. There never was such a struggle in any age or any country. Why? Because the President and all under him did repeatedly and distinctly declare that the sole purpose was to uphold the Constitution which our fathers had made and the Union which that Constitution established, and to which we owed all our greatness and prosperity.

The people of America were willing to sacrifice all these for that great good. It was so said in the President's annual message of the 4th of July, as it had been in his proclamation of the 15th of April, calling forth the militia, in the beginning. It was in the orders and proclamations of every Federal general for the first eight or ten months after he entered the Southern states. The day after the Battle of Bull Run, by a vote unanimous save two, Congress declared that the sole purpose of the war should be the maintenance of the Constitution, the restoration of the Union, and the enforcement of the laws; and when these objects were accomplished, the war should cease, without touching the domestic institutions, slavery included, in the Southern states. That pledge was given, and under it an army of 600,000 men was at once raised; and it was repeated in every form till toward the close of the second session of Congress. Then the Abolition senators and representatives began first to demand a change in the policy of the administration, they began to proclaim that the war must be no longer for the Union and the Constitution but for the abolition of slavery in the Southern states.

Now, sir, I repeat it and defy contradiction, that not a soldier enlisted, out of the first 900,000, for any other purpose than the restoration of the Union and the maintenance of the Constitution. There was not one single officer, so far as his public declarations were concerned, whatever may have been the secret purposes of his heart, that did not openly declare that the moment this object was changed to the abolition of slavery, he would throw up his commission and resign. Yes, the very men who, for the last four or five weeks in the army—the officers—I do not mean your private soldiers, they who do picket duty, who stand in the front ranks, who brave the iron hail and leaden rain of the stormy battlefield, the men who sacrifice their lives for the paltry sum of $13 a month, the noble, brave men, who, if they were at home, would give us their votes, as their sympathies are still with us; I speak of your officers only—your majors, your lieutenant colonels, colonels, brigadiers, and major generals, each one of them seeking promotion, and drawing his salary of $2,000, $3,000, $4,000, $5,000, $6,000, and $7,000 a year, and whose interest it is that the war be made eternal.

They are the men who have been holding these meetings of regiments so-called, concocting resolutions, or rather adopting resolutions concocted in Indianapolis, Columbus, Springfield, or Washington, and sent down to be clothed in form as an expression of the opinion of the regiments, but, in fact, the expression of the officers alone. They are the men who have solemnly declared, at home and in the Army, that the moment this became an Abolition war, they would resign and come back to us, and yet they are now sending out these missiles to us their peers—threatening messages that they mean to come back and "whip" the Democratic traitors and secessionists of the North.

Now, I tell these shoulder-strapped gentlemen who are looking to the White House instead of at the enemy that when they have succeeded in the mission for which they were sent out; when upon the battlefield they have put down those who are now in arms against them, it will be time enough to talk about coming back. But if they imagine for one moment that any man here is to be frightened by their insolent messages, they know not the spirit of the freemen who remain at home. ...

If there be any man in the Democratic or Republican Party who still thinks that war can restore the Union as it was and maintain the Constitution as it is, I have no quarrel with him tonight. I assume his position for the sake of argument—it is not mine, and never was; but let it be so for a moment. You say that a war prosecuted for this purpose must thus result. Have you the power to change the purpose? Can you compel Abraham Lincoln to withdraw his proclamation? Can you repeal the legislation of the Congress that is now defunct? If you cannot, the war must go on upon the basis on which it is now prosecuted—and you believe that it will end in death to the Union, the Constitution, and to liberty.

What position, then, do you occupy before your countrymen in still advocating the so-called vigorous prosecution of the war? Vigorous prosecution! For what? By your own declaration—disunion, separation, destruction, despotism. Dare any man stand before an assembly of freemen and advocate the objects or the results, at least, of such a war? And yet what inconsistency for anyone claiming intelligence to declare that although it must so result,

and although he has not the power to change the policy of the administration, it is the duty of every man to support that administration in its policy. I deny it; and for one, at least, I will not do it. If I had believed originally, as I did not believe, that it was possible to restore this Union by force, if I had occupied the position of hundreds and thousands of Democrats, as well as the great mass of the Republican Party, I would proclaim tonight that, inasmuch as this is the policy and we have not the power to change it, that then our duty would be, and is, to advocate henceforth to the end a vigorous prosecution of peace for the Union.

I will not consent to put the entire purse of the country and the sword of the country into the hands of the executive, giving him despotic and dictatorial power to carry out an object which I avow before my countrymen is the destruction of their liberties and the overthrow of the Union of these states. I do not comprehend the honesty of such declarations or of the men who make them. I know that the charge is brought against myself, personally, and against many of us. I have not spent a moment in replying to it—the people will take care of all that.

The charge has been made against us—all who are opposed to the policy of this administration and opposed to this war—that we are for "peace on any terms." It is false, I am not, but I am for an immediate stopping of the war and for honorable peace. I am for peace for the sake of the Union of these states. More than that—I am for peace, and would be, even if the

Union could not be restored, as I believe it can be; because without peace, permitting this administration for two years to exercise its tremendous powers, the war still existing, you will not have one remnant of civil liberty left among yourselves. The exercise of these tremendous powers, the apology for which is the existence of this war, is utterly incompatible with the stability of the Constitution and of constitutional liberty.

I am not for "peace on any terms"; I would not be with any country on the globe. Honor is also the life of the nation, and it is never to be sacrificed. I have as high and proud a sense of honor, and have a right to have it, as any man in the South, and I love my country too well, and cherish its honor too profoundly, for one single moment to consent to a dishonorable peace. Yes, the whole country; every state; and I, unlike some of my own party, and unlike thousands of the Abolition Party, believe still, before God, that the Union can be reconstructed and will be. That is my faith, and I mean to cling to it as the wrecked mariner clings to the last plank amid the shipwreck. But when I see that the experiment of blood has failed from the beginning, as I believed it would fail, I am not one of those who proclaim now that we shall have separation and disunion. I am for going back to the instrumentality through which this Union was first made, and by which alone it can be restored.

I am for peace, because it is the first step toward conciliation and compromise. You cannot move until you have first taken that indispensable preliminary—a cessation of hostilities. But it is said that the South has refused to accept or listen to any terms whatever. How do you know that? Has it been tried? Now, gentlemen, I know very well what the papers in support of the administration at Richmond say. I know what men in the Senate and House of Representatives at Richmond declare on this subject; I have read it all. We are indebted to the Abolition papers for the republication of all that. But I do hope that no man who has ever known me in person or by speech supposed for one moment that I expected that the children of that revolution, the men who sprang from it, the men who are dependent upon it, or even the men holding power now under it would, while this war lasted, listen to any terms of settlement. I would as soon expect Abraham Lincoln and his cabinet to propose such terms on the basis of the Union of fifty years ago as Jefferson Davis or any man in Richmond.

Now I am not, perhaps, the most sensitive man in the world, and yet I have a reasonable degree of sensitiveness and, I hope, some common sense with it; but I do not feel, as I am afraid some of our friends do feel, personally slighted, because, while I have advocated a peaceable settlement of our difficultie —conciliation and compromise for the restoration of the Union of these states—I have met with opposition and with hostility from the papers in Richmond. I did not look for it, gentlemen, although I have a better right to it than some of your friends here from my former relation to the Democratic Party of the South, when they were acknowledging obedience to the Constitution and were still in the Union; but I did not expect that Jefferson Davis, and Benjamin, and Hunter, or any of them would, when I opened my arms and said, "Return, prodigal sons," rush with tears to my embrace—and I do not feel hurt. I am not the least "miffed" by it; and I certainly shall not therefore advocate a vigorous prosecution of the war to punish them.

I am afraid some gentlemen imagined, when they gave out this invitation, that it would be, of course, accepted at once; although one of those who first proclaimed it had even less power than I have, certainly not more—and was very much in the condition of that distinguished personage who, from the top of a certain high mountain, promised all the kingdoms of the world. I do not think that he or I, or any other man while this administration is in place, has the power to conciliate and compromise now.

Take the theory for what it is worth, and let men of intelligence judge; let history attest it hereafter. My theory upon that subject, then, is this—stop this war.

PATRIOTIC SONGS OF NORTH AND SOUTH

Source: *Heart Songs*, Cleveland, 1909. *War Songs and Poems of the Southern Confederacy 1861-1865*, H.M. Wharton, ed., n.p., 1904.

THE BATTLE-CRY OF FREEDOM

Yes, we'll rally round the flag, boys, we'll rally once again,
Shouting the battle-cry of freedom,
We will rally from the hillside, we'll gather from the plain,
Shouting the battle-cry of freedom.

Chorus:
The Union forever, hurrah! boys, hurrah!
Down with the traitor, up with the star,
While we rally round the flag, boys, rally once again,
Shouting the battle-cry of freedom.

We are springing to the call of our brothers gone before,
Shouting the battle-cry of freedom,
And we'll fill the vacant ranks with a million freemen more,
Shouting the battle-cry of freedom.

We will welcome to our numbers the loyal, true, and brave,
Shouting the battle-cry of freedom,
And although they may be poor, not a man shall be a slave,
Shouting the battle-cry of freedom.

So we're springing to the call from the East and from the West,
Shouting the battle-cry of freedom,
And we'll hurl the rebel crew from the land we love the best,
Shouting the battle-cry of freedom.

George Frederick Root

THE BONNIE BLUE FLAG

We are a band of brothers
And native to the soil,
Fighting for the property
We gained by honest toil;
And when our rights were
threatened,
The cry rose near and far —
"Hurrah for the Bonnie Blue Flag
That bears the single star!"

Chorus:
Hurrah! hurrah!
For Southern rights, hurrah!
Hurrah for the Bonnie Blue Flag
That bears the single star.

As long as the Union
Was faithful to her trust,
Like friends and like brothers
Both kind were we and just;
But now, when Northern treachery
Attempts our rights to mar,
We hoist on high the Bonnie Blue Flag
That bears the single star.

First gallant South Carolina
Nobly made the stand,
Then came Alabama,
Who took her by the hand;
Next quickly Mississippi,
Georgia and Florida,
All raised on high the Bonnie Blue Flag
That bears the single star.

And here's to old Virginia —
The Old Dominion State —
With the young Confed'racy

At length has linked her fate.
Impelled by her example,
Now other states prepare
To hoist on high the Bonnie Blue Flag
That bears the single star.

Then here's to our Confed'racy,
Strong are we and brave,
Like patriots of old we'll fight
Our heritage to save.
And rather than submit to shame,
To die we would prefer;
So cheer for the Bonnie Blue Flag
That bears the single star.

Then cheer, boys, cheer;
Raise the joyous shout,
For Arkansas and North Carolina
Now have both gone out;
And let another rousing cheer
For Tennessee be given,
The single star of the Bonnie Blue Flag
Has grown to be eleven.

Harry McCarty

ABRAHAM LINCOLN: SECOND INAUGURAL ADDRESS (1865)

Source: *Complete Works of Abraham Lincoln*, John G. Nicolay and John Hay, eds., New York, 1905, Vol. XI, pp. 44–47.

At this second appearing to take the oath of the presidential office, there is less occasion for an extended address than there was at the first. Then, a statement, somewhat in detail, of a course to be pursued seemed fitting and proper. Now, at the expiration of four years, during which public declarations have been constantly called forth on every point and phase of the great contest which still absorbs the attention and engrosses the energies of the nation, little that is new could be presented. The progress of our arms, upon which all else chiefly depends, is as well known to the public as to myself, and it is, I trust, reasonably satisfactory and encouraging to all. With high hope for the future, no prediction in regard to it is ventured.

On the occasion corresponding to this four years ago, all thoughts were anxiously directed to an impending civil war. All dreaded it, all sought to avert it. While the inaugural address was being delivered from this place, devoted altogether to saving the Union without war, insurgent agents were in the city seeking to destroy it without war—seeking to dissolve the Union and divide effects by negotiation. Both parties deprecated war, but one of them would make war rather than let the nation survive, and the other would accept war rather than let it perish. And the war came.

One-eighth of the whole population were colored slaves, not distributed generally over the Union but localized in the southern part of it. These slaves constituted a peculiar and powerful interest. All knew that this interest was somehow the cause of the war. To strengthen, perpetuate, and extend this interest was the object for which the insurgents would rend the Union, even by war, while the government claimed no right to do more

than to restrict the territorial enlargement of it.

Neither party expected for the war the magnitude or the duration which it has already attained. Neither anticipated that the cause of the conflict might cease with or even before the conflict itself should cease. Each looked for an easier triumph and a result less fundamental and astounding. Both read the same Bible and pray to the same God, and each invokes His aid against the other.

It may seem strange that any men should dare to ask a just God's assistance in wringing their bread from the sweat of other men's faces, but let us judge not that we be not judged. The prayers of both could not be answered. That of neither has been answered fully. The Almighty has His own purposes. "Woe unto the world because of offenses! for it must needs be that offenses come; but woe to that man by whom the offense cometh."

If we shall suppose that American slavery is one of those offenses which, in the providence of God, must needs come, but which, having continued through His appointed time, He now wills to remove, and that He gives to both North and South this terrible war as the woe due to those by whom the offense came, shall we discern therein any departure from those divine attributes which the believers in a living God always ascribe to Him? Fondly do we hope, fervently do we pray, that this mighty scourge of war may speedily pass away.

Yet, if God wills that it continue until all the wealth piled by the bondsman's

250 years of unrequited toil shall be sunk, and until every drop of blood drawn with the lash shall be paid by another drawn with the sword, as was said 3,000 years ago, so still it must be said, "The judgments of the Lord are true and righteous altogether."

With malice toward none, with charity for all, with firmness in the right as God gives us to see the right, let us strive on to finish the work we are in, to bind up the nation's wounds, to care for him who shall have borne the battle and for his widow and his orphan—to do all which may achieve and cherish a just and lasting peace among ourselves and with all nations.

GEORGE E. PICKETT: THE NIGHT BEFORE APPOMATTOX (1865)

Source: *Soldier of the South, General Pickett's War Letters to His Wife*, Arthur C. Inman, ed., Boston, 1928, pp. 134–137.

I would have your life, my darling, all sunshine, all brightness. I would have no sorrow, no pain, no fear come to you but all

To be as cloudless, save with rare and roseate shadows
As I would thy fate.

And yet the very thoughts of me that come to you must bring all that I would spare you.

Tomorrow may see our flag furled, forever.

Jackerie, our faithful old mail carrier, sobs behind me as I write. He bears tonight this—his last—message from me to you. He is commissioned with three orders, which I know you will obey as fearlessly as the bravest of your brother soldiers. Keep up a stout heart. Believe that I shall come back to you. Know that God reigns. After tonight, you will be my whole command—staff, field officers, men—all.

Lee's surrender is imminent. It is finished. Through the suggestion of their commanding officers as many of the men as desire are permitted to cut through and join Johnston's army. The cloud of despair settled over all on the 3rd, when the tidings came to us of the evacuation of Richmond and its partial loss by fire. The homes and families of many of my men were there, and all knew too well that with the fall of our capital, the last hope of success was over. And yet, my beloved, these men as resolutely obeyed the orders of their commanding officers as if we had just captured and burned the Federal capitol.

The horrors of the march from Five Forks to Amelia Court House, and thence to Sailor's Creek, beggar all description. For forty-eight hours the man or officer who had a handful of parched corn in his pocket was most fortunate. We reached Sailor's Creek on the morning of the 6th— weary, starving, despairing.

Sheridan was in our front, delaying us with his cavalry, according to his custom, until the infantry should come up. Mahone was on our right; Ewell on our left. Mahone was ordered to move on, and we were ordered to stand still. The movement of Mahone left a gap which increased as he went on. Huger's battalion of artillery, in attempting to cross the gap, was being swept away, when I pushed on with two of my brigades across Sailor's Creek.

We formed line of battle across an open field, holding it against repeated charges of Sheridan's dismounted cavalry. At about 3 o'clock, the infantry which Sheridan had been looking for came up, completely hemming us in. Anderson ordered me to draw off my brigades to the rear and to cut our way out in any possible manner that we could. Wise's brigade was deployed in the rear to assist us but was charged upon on all sides by the enemy, and, though fighting manfully to the last, was forced to yield. Two of my brigadiers, Corse and Hunton, were taken prisoners. The other two barely escaped, and my life, by some miracle, was spared. And by another miracle, greater still, I escaped capture.

A squadron of the enemy's cavalry was riding down upon us, two of my staff and myself, when a small squad of my men recognized me and, risking their own lives, rallied to our assistance and suddenly delivered a last volley into the faces of the pursuing horsemen, checking them for a moment. But in that one moment we, by the speed of our horses, made our escape. Ah, my darling, the sacrifice of that little band of men was like unto that which was made at Calvary.

It is finished! Ah, my beloved division! Thousands of them have gone to their eternal home, having given up their lives for the cause they knew to be just. The others, alas, heartbroken, crushed in spirit, are left to mourn its loss. Well, it is practically all over now. We have poured out our blood, and suffered untold hardships and privations, all in vain. And now, well—*I* must not forget, either, that God reigns.

> *Blackguard and buffoon as [Lincoln] is, he has pursued his end with an energy as untiring as an Indian and a singleness of purpose that might almost be called patriotic.*

Anon., in the *Charleston Mercury*, Jan. 10, 1865

WALT WHITMAN: COME UP FROM THE FIELDS FATHER (1865)

Source: *Leaves of Grass*, New York, 1867.

COME UP FROM THE FIELDS FATHER

Come up from the fields father, here's a letter from our Pete, And come to the front door mother, here's a letter from thy dear son.

Lo, 'tis autumn, Lo, where the trees, deeper green, yellower and redder,

Cool and sweeten Ohio's villages with leaves fluttering in the moderate wind,
Where apples ripe in the orchards hang and grapes on the trellised vines,
(Smell you the smell of the grapes on the vines?
Smell you the buckwheat where the bees were lately buzzing?)

Above all, lo, the sky so calm, so transparent after the rain, and with wondrous clouds,
Below too, all calm, all vital and beautiful, and the farm prospers well.

Down in the fields all prospers well,
But now from the fields come father, come at the daughter's call,
And come to the entry mother, to the front door come right away

Fast as she can she hurries, something ominous, her steps trembling,
She does not tarry to smooth her hair nor adjust her cap.

Open the envelope quickly,
O this is not our son's writing, yet his name is signed,
O a strange hand writes for our dear son, O stricken mother's soul!
All swims before her eyes, flashes with black, she catches the main words only,

Sentences broken, gunshot wound in the breast, cavalry skirmish, taken to hospital,

At present low, but will soon be better.

Ah now the single figure to me,
Amid all teeming and wealthy Ohio with all its cities and farms,
Sickly white in the face and dull in the head, very faint,
By the jamb of a door leans.

Grieve not so, dear mother (the just grown daughter speaks through her sobs,
The little sisters huddle around speechless and dismayed),

See, dearest mother, the letter says Pete will soon be better.

Alas poor boy, he will never be better (nor maybe needs to be better, that brave and simple soul),
While they stand at home at the door he is dead already,
The only son is dead.

But the mother needs to be better,
She with thin form presently dressed in black,
By day her meals untouched, then at night fitfully sleeping, often waking,
In the midnight waking, weeping, longing with one deep longing,

*O that she might withdraw unno-
ticed, silent from life escape and
withdraw,
To follow, to seek, to be with her
dear dead son.*

FRANK WILKESON:
HOW AMERICANS DIE
IN BATTLE (1864)

Source: *Recollections of a Private Soldier
in the Army of the Potomac*, New York,
1887: "How Men Die in Battle."

Almost every death on the battlefield
is different. And the manner of the death
depends on the wound and on the man,
whether he is cowardly or brave, whether
his vitality is large or small, whether he is
a man of active imagination or is dull of
intellect, whether he is of nervous or lymphatic temperament. I instance deaths
and wounds that I saw in Grant's last
campaign.

On the second day of the Battle of
the Wilderness, where I fought as an
infantry soldier, I saw more men killed
and wounded than I did before or after
in the same time. I knew but few of the
men in the regiment in whose ranks I
stood; but I learned the Christian names
of some of them.

The man who stood next to me on my
right was called Will. He was cool, brave,
and intelligent. In the morning, when
Corps II was advancing and driving Hill's
soldiers slowly back, I was flurried. He
noticed it and steadied my nerves by saying, kindly: "Don't fire so fast. This fight
will last all day. Don't hurry. Cover your

man before you pull the trigger. Take it
easy, my boy, take it easy, and your cartridges will last the longer." This man
fought effectively. During the day I had
learned to look up to this excellent soldier and lean on him.

Toward evening, as we were being
slowly driven back to the Brock Road by
Longstreet's men, we made a stand. I was
behind a tree firing, with my rifle barrel
resting on the stub of a limb. Will was
standing by my side, but in the open. He,
with a groan, doubled up and dropped on
the ground at my feet. He looked up at me.
His face was pale. He gasped for breath
a few times, and then said faintly: "That
ends me. I am shot through the bowels."
I said: "Crawl to the rear. We are not far
from the entrenchments along the Brock
Road." I saw him sit up and indistinctly
saw him reach for his rifle, which had
fallen from his hands as he fell. Again I
spoke to him, urging him to go to the rear.
He looked at me and said impatiently: "I
tell you that I am as good as dead. There
is no use in fooling with me. I shall stay
here." Then he pitched forward dead, shot
again and through the head. We fell back
before Longstreet's soldiers and left Will
lying in a windrow of dead men.

When we got into the Brock Road
entrenchments, a man a few files to my
left dropped dead, shot just above the
right eye. He did not groan, or sigh, or
make the slightest physical movement,
except that his chest heaved a few times.
The life went out of his face instantly,
leaving it without a particle of expression.
It was plastic and, as the facial muscles

contracted, it took many shapes. When this man's body became cold and his face hardened, it was horribly distorted, as though he had suffered intensely. Any person who had not seen him killed would have said that he had endured supreme agony before death released him. A few minutes after he fell, another man, a little farther to the left, fell with apparently a precisely similar wound. He was straightened out and lived for over an hour. He did not speak, simply lay on his back, and his broad chest rose and fell, slowly at first, and then faster and faster, and more and more feebly, until he was dead. And his face hardened, and it was almost terrifying in its painful distortion. I have seen dead soldiers' faces which were wreathed in smiles and heard their comrades say that they had died happy.

I do not believe that the face of a dead soldier, lying on a battlefield, ever truthfully indicates the mental or physical anguish, or peacefulness of mind, which he suffered or enjoyed before his death. The face is plastic after death, and as the facial muscles cool and contract, they draw the face into many shapes. Sometimes the dead smile, again they stare with glassy eyes, and lolling tongues, and dreadfully distorted visages at you. It goes for nothing. One death was as painless as the other.

After Longstreet's soldiers had driven Corps II into their entrenchments along the Brock Road, a battle-exhausted infantryman stood behind a large oak tree. His back rested against it. He was very tired and held his rifle loosely in his hand. The Confederates were directly in our front. This soldier was apparently in perfect safety. A solid shot from a Confederate gun struck the oak tree squarely about four feet from the ground; but it did not have sufficient force to tear through the tough wood. The soldier fell dead. There was not a scratch on him. He was killed by concussion.

While we were fighting savagely over these entrenchments, the woods in our front caught fire, and I saw many of our wounded burned to death. Must they not have suffered horribly? I am not at all sure of that. The smoke rolled heavily and slowly before the fire. It enveloped the wounded, and I think that by far the larger portion of the men who were roasted were suffocated before the flames curled round them. The spectacle was courage-sapping and pitiful, and it appealed strongly to the imagination of the spectators; but I do not believe that the wounded soldiers, who were being burned, suffered greatly, if they suffered at all.

Wounded soldiers, it mattered not how slight the wounds, generally hastened away from the battle lines. A wound entitled a man to go to the rear and to a hospital. Of course there were many exceptions to this rule, as there would necessarily be in battles where from 20,000 to 30,000 men were wounded. I frequently saw slightly wounded men who were marching with their colors. I personally saw but two men wounded who continued to fight.

During the first day's fighting in the Wilderness, I saw a youth of about twenty years skip and yell, stung by a bullet through the thigh. He turned to limp to the rear. After he had gone a few steps he stopped, then he kicked out his leg once or twice to see if it would work. Then he tore the clothing away from his leg so as to see the wound. He looked at it attentively for an instant, then kicked out his leg again, then turned and took his place in the ranks and resumed firing. There was considerable disorder in the line, and the soldiers moved to and fro—now a few feet to the right, now a few feet to the left. One of these movements brought me directly behind this wounded soldier. I could see plainly from that position, and I pushed into the gaping line and began firing. In a minute or two the wounded soldier dropped his rifle and, clasping his left arm, exclaimed: "I am hit again!" He sat down behind the battle ranks and tore off the sleeve of his shirt. The wound was very slight—not much more than skin-deep. He tied his handkerchief around it, picked up his rifle, and took position alongside of me. I said: "You are fighting in bad luck today. You had better get away from here." He turned his head to answer me. His head jerked, he staggered, then fell, then regained his feet. A tiny fountain of blood and teeth and bone and bits of tongue burst out of his mouth. He had been shot through the jaws; the lower one was broken and hung down. I looked directly into his open mouth, which was ragged and bloody and tongueless. He cast his rifle furiously on the ground and staggered off.

The next day, just before Longstreet's soldiers made their first charge on Corps II, I heard the peculiar cry a stricken man utters as the bullet tears through his flesh. I turned my head, as I loaded my rifle, to see who was hit. I saw a bearded Irishman pull up his shirt. He had been wounded in the left side just below the floating ribs. His face was gray with fear. The wound looked as though it were mortal. He looked at it for an instant, then poked it gently with his index finger. He flushed redly and smiled with satisfaction. He tucked his shirt into his trousers and was fighting in the ranks again before I had capped my rifle. The ball had cut a groove in his skin only. The play of this Irishman's face was so expressive, his emotions changed so quickly, that I could not keep from laughing.

Near Spotsylvania I saw, as my battery was moving into action, a group of wounded men lying in the shade cast by some large oak trees. All of these men's faces were gray. They silently looked at us as we marched past them. One wounded man, a blond giant of about forty years, was smoking a short briarwood pipe. He had a firm grip on the pipestem. I asked him what he was doing. "Having my last smoke, young fellow," he replied. His dauntless blue eyes met mine, and he bravely tried to smile. I saw that he was dying fast. Another of these wounded men was trying to read a letter. He was too weak to hold it, or maybe his sight was clouded. He thrust it unread into the breast pocket of his blouse and lay back with a moan.

This group of wounded men numbered fifteen or twenty. At the time, I thought that all of them were fatally wounded and that there was no use in the surgeons wasting time on them, when men who could be saved were clamoring for their skillful attention. None of these soldiers cried aloud, none called on wife, or mother, or father. They lay on the ground, palefaced, and with set jaws, waiting for their end. They moaned and groaned as they suffered, but none of them flunked. When my battery returned from the front, five or six hours afterward, almost all of these men were dead. Long before the campaign was over I concluded that dying soldiers seldom called on those who were dearest to them, seldom conjured their Northern or Southern homes, until they became delirious. Then, when their minds wandered and fluttered at the approach of freedom, they babbled of their homes. Some were boys again and were fishing in Northern trout streams. Some were generals leading their men to victory. Some were with their wives and children. Some wandered over their family's homestead; but all, with rare exceptions, were delirious.

At the North Anna River, my battery being in action, an infantry soldier, one of our supports, who was lying face downward close behind the gun I served on, and in a place where he thought he was safe, was struck on the thighs by a large jagged piece of a shell. The wound made by this fragment of iron was as horrible as any I saw in the army. The flesh of both thighs was torn off, exposing the bones. The soldier bled to death in a few minutes, and before he died he conjured his Northern home, and murmured of his wife and children.

In the same battle, but on the south side of the river, a man who carried a rifle was passing between the guns and caissons of the battery. A solid shot, intended for us, struck him on the side. His entire bowels were torn out and slung in ribbons and shreds on the ground. He fell dead, but his arms and legs jerked convulsively a few times. It was a sickening spectacle. During this battle I saw a Union picket knocked down, probably by a rifle ball striking his head and glancing from it. He lay as though dead. Presently, he struggled to his feet, and, with blood streaming from his head, he staggered aimlessly round and round in a circle, as sheep afflicted with grubs in the brain do. Instantly, the Confederate sharpshooters opened fire on him and speedily killed him as he circled.

Wounded soldiers almost always tore their clothing away from their wounds so as to see them and to judge of their character. Many of them would smile and their faces would brighten as they realized that they were not hard hit and that they could go home for a few months. Others would give a quick glance at their wounds and then shrink back as from a blow, and turn pale as they realized the truth that they were mortally wounded. The enlisted men were exceedingly accurate judges of the probable result which would ensue from any wound they saw. They had seen hundreds of soldiers wounded, and they had noticed that certain wounds always resulted fatally. They knew when they were fatally wounded, and after the shock of discovery had passed, they generally braced themselves and died in a manly manner. It was seldom that an American or Irish volunteer flunked in the presence of death.

CIVIL RIGHTS ACT (1866)

Source: *The Public Statutes at Large of the United States of America from the Organization of the Government in 1789, etc., etc.,* Vol. XIV, pp. 27–29.

An Act to Protect all Persons in the United States in their Civil Rights, and Furnish the Means of their Vindication.

Be it enacted by the Senate and House of Representatives of the United States of America in Congress assembled, that all persons born in the United States and not subject to any foreign power, excluding Indians not taxed, are hereby declared to be citizens of the United States; and such citizens, of every race and color, without regard to any previous condition of slavery or involuntary servitude, except as a punishment for crime whereof the party shall have been duly convicted, shall have the same right, in every state and territory in the United States, to make and enforce contracts; to sue; be parties, and give evidence; to inherit, purchase, lease, sell, hold, and convey real and personal property; and to full and equal benefit of all laws and proceedings for the security of person and property as is enjoyed by white citizens, and shall be subject to like

punishment, pains, and penalties, and to none other, any law, statute, ordinance, regulation, or custom to the contrary notwithstanding.

Section 2. *And be it further enacted,* that any person who, under color of any law, statute, ordinance, regulation, or custom, shall subject, or cause to be subjected, any inhabitant of any state or territory to the deprivation of any right secured or protected by this act, or to different punishment, pains, or penalties on account of such person having at any time been held in a condition of slavery or involuntary servitude, except as a punishment for crime whereof the party shall have been duly convicted, or by reason of his color or race, than is prescribed for the punishment of white persons, shall be deemed guilty of a misdemeanor, and, on conviction, shall be punished by fine not exceeding $1,000 or imprisonment not exceeding one year, or both, in the discretion of the court.

Section 3. *And be it further enacted,* that the district courts of the United States, within their respective districts, shall have, exclusively of the courts of the several states, cognizance of all crimes and offenses committed against the provisions of this act, and also, concurrently with the circuit courts of the United States, of all causes, civil and criminal, affecting persons who are denied or cannot enforce in the courts or judicial tribunals of the state or locality where they may be any of the rights secured to them by the 1st Section of this act; and if any suit or prosecution, civil or criminal, has been or shall be commenced in any state court, against any such person, for any cause whatsoever, or against any officer, civil or military, or other person, for any arrest or imprisonment, trespasses, or wrongs done or committed by virtue or under color of authority derived from this act or the act establishing a bureau for the relief of freedmen and refugees, and all acts amendatory thereof, or for refusing to do any act upon the ground that it would be inconsistent with this act, such defendant shall have the right to remove such cause for trial to the proper district or circuit court in the manner prescribed by the "Act relating to habeas corpus and regulating judicial proceedings in certain cases," approved March 3, 1863, and all acts amendatory thereof. ...

Section 4. *And be it further enacted*, that the district attorneys, marshals, and deputy marshals of the United States, the commissioners appointed by the circuit and territorial courts of the United States, with powers of arresting, imprisoning, or bailing offenders against the laws of the United States, the officers and agents of the Freedmen's Bureau, and every other officer who may be specially empowered by the President of the United States, shall be, and they are hereby, specially authorized and required, at the expense of the United States, to institute proceedings against all and every person who shall violate the provisions of this act, and cause him or them to be arrested and imprisoned, or bailed, as the case may be, for trial before such court of the United States or territorial court as by this act has cognizance of the offense.

And with a view to affording reasonable protection to all persons in their constitutional rights of equality before the law, without distinction of race or color, or previous condition of slavery or involuntary servitude, except as a punishment for crime, whereof the party shall have been duly convicted, and to the prompt discharge of the duties of this act, it shall be the duty of the circuit courts of the United States and the superior courts of the territories of the United States, from time to time, to increase the number of commissioners so as to afford a speedy and convenient means for the arrest and examination of persons charged with a violation of this act; and such commissioners are hereby authorized and required to exercise and discharge all the powers and duties conferred on them by this act, and the same duties with regard to offenses created by this act, as they are authorized by law to exercise with regard to other offenses against the laws of the United States. ...

Section 8. *And be it further enacted*, that whenever the President of the United States shall have reason to believe that offenses have been or are likely to be committed against the provisions of this act within any judicial district, it shall be lawful for him, in his discretion, to direct the judge, marshal, and district attorney of such district to attend at such place within the district, and for such time as he may designate, for the purpose of the more speedy arrest and trial of persons charged with a violation of this act; and it shall be the duty of every judge or other officer, when any such requisition shall be received by him, to attend at the place and for the time therein designated.

Section 9. *And be it further enacted,* that it shall be lawful for the President of the United States, or such person as he may empower for that purpose, to employ such part of the land or naval forces of the United States, or of the militia, as shall be necessary to prevent the violation and enforce the due execution of this act.

Section 10. *And be it further enacted,* that, upon all questions of law arising in any cause under the provisions of this act, a final appeal may be taken to the Supreme Court of the United States.

ANDREW JOHNSON: AGAINST THE RADICAL REPUBLICANS (1866)

Source: *New York Herald*, Feb. 23, 1866.

I have already remarked that there were two parties—one for destroying the government to preserve slavery, and the other to break up the government to destroy slavery. The objects to be accomplished were different, it is true, so far as slavery is concerned, but they agreed in one thing, and that was the breaking up of the government. They agreed in the destruction of the government, the precise thing which I have already stood up to oppose. Whether the disunionists come from the South or the North, I stand now where I did then, to vindicate the Union

of these states and the Constitution of the country. ...

Who, I ask, has suffered more for the Union than I have? I shall not now repeat the wrongs or suffering inflicted upon me; but it is not the way to deal with a whole people in the spirit of revenge. ... There is no one who has labored harder than I have to have the principal conscious and intelligent traitors brought to justice; to have the law vindicated, and the great fact vindicated that treason is a crime. Yet, while conscious, intelligent traitors are to be punished, should whole states, communities, and people be made to submit to and bear the penalty of death? I have, perhaps, as much hostility and as much resentment as a man ought to have; but we should conform our action and our conduct to the example of Him who founded our holy religion. ...

But, gentlemen, I came into power under the Constitution of the country and by the approbation of the people. And what did I find? I found 8 million people who were, in fact, condemned under the law—and the penalty was death. Under the idea of revenge and resentment, they were to be annihilated and destroyed. ...

Let them repent and let them acknowledge their allegiance. Let them become loyal and willing supporters and defenders of our glorious stripes and stars and the Constitution of our country. *Let their leaders, the conscious, intelligent traitors, suffer the penalty of the law*; but for the great mass who have been forced into this rebellion and misled by their leaders, I say *leniency, kindness, trust, and confidence.*

But, my countrymen, after having passed through the rebellion and given such evidence as I have—though men croak a great deal about it now—when I look back through the battlefields and see many of these brave men, in whose company I was in part of the rebellion where it was most difficult and doubtful to be found—before the smoke of battle has scarcely passed away; before the blood has scarcely congealed—what do we find? The rebellion is put down by the strong arm of the government in the field, *but is it the only way in which we can have rebellion?* They struggled for the breaking up of the government, but before they are scarcely out of the battlefield, and before our brave men have scarcely returned to their houses to renew the ties of affection and love, we find ourselves almost *in the midst of another rebellion.*

The war to suppress our rebellion was to prevent the separation of the states and thereby change the character of the government and weakening its power. Now, what is the change? There is an attempt to concentrate the power of the government in the hands of a few, and *thereby bring about consolidation which is equally dangerous and objectionable with separation.* We find that powers are assumed and attempted to be exercised of a most extraordinary character. What are they? We find that *governments can be revolutionized, can be changed without going into the battlefield.* ...

Now, what are the attempts? What is being proposed? We find that, in fact, by an irresponsible central directory, nearly all the powers of government are assumed without even consulting the legislative or executive departments of the government. Yes, and by resolution, reported by a committee upon whom all the legislative power of the government has been conferred, that principle in the Constitution which authorizes and empowers each branch of the Legislative Department to be judges of the election and qualifications of its own members has been virtually taken away from those departments and conferred upon a committee, who must report before they can act under the Constitution and allow members duly elected to take their seats. By this rule they assume that there must be laws passed; that there must be recognition in respect to a state in the Union, with all its practical relations restored before the respective houses of Congress, under the Constitution, shall judge of the election and qualifications of its own members.

What position is that? You have been struggling for four years to put down the rebellion. You denied in the beginning of the struggle that any state had the right to go out. You said that they had neither the right nor the power. The issue has been made, and it has been settled that a state has neither the right nor the power to go out of the Union. And when you have settled that by the executive and military power of the government and by the public judgment, you *turn around and assume that they are out and shall not come in.*

I am free to say to you, as your Executive, that *I am not prepared to take any such position.* I said in the Senate, at the very inception of the rebellion, that states had no right to go out and that they had no power to go out. That question has been settled. And I cannot turn round now and give the direct lie to all I profess to have done in the last five years. I can do no such thing. I say that when these states comply with the Constitution, when they have given sufficient evidence of their loyalty and that they can be trusted, when they yield obedience to the law, I say, *extend to them the right band of fellowship,* and let peace and union be restored.

I have fought traitors and treason in the South; I opposed the Davises and [the] Toombses, the Slidells, and a long list of others whose names I need not repeat; and now, when I turn around at the other end of the line, I find men—I care not by what name you call them—who still stand opposed to the restoration of the Union of these states; and I am free to say to you that I am still for the preservation of this compact; I am still for the restoration of this Union; I am still in favor of this great government of ours going on and following out its destiny.

A gentleman calls for their names. Well, suppose I should give them. I look upon them—I repeat it, as President or citizen—as being as much opposed to the fundamental principles of the government and believe they are as much laboring to prevent or destroy them as were the men who fought against us. *I say*

Thaddeus Stevens of Pennsylvania; I say Charles Summer; I say Wendell Phillips and others of the same stripe are among them. Some gentleman in the crowd says, "Give it to Forney." I have only just to say that *I do not waste my ammunition upon dead ducks.* I stand for my country, I stand for the Constitution, where I placed my feet from my entrance into public life. They may traduce me, they may slander me, they may vituperate; but let me say to you that it has no effect upon me. And let me say in addition that *I do not intend to be bullied by my enemies.*

I know, my countrymen, that it has been insinuated, and not only insinuated but said directly—the intimation has been given in high places—that if such a usurpation of power had been exercised 200 years ago in a particular reign, it would have cost a certain individual his head. What usurpation has Andrew Johnson been guilty of? The usurpation I have been guilty of has always been standing between the people and the encroachments of power. And because I dared to say in a conversation with a fellow citizen, and a senator too, that I thought amendments to the Constitution ought not to be so frequent; that their effect would be that it would lose all its dignity; that the old instrument would be lost sight of in a short time—because I happened to say that if it was amended such and such amendments should be adopted, it was a usurpation of power that would have cost a king his head at a certain time.

And in connection with this subject it was explained by the same gentleman that we were in the midst of an earth-quake; that he trembled and could not yield. Yes, *there is an earthquake coming. There is a ground swell coming of popular judgment and indignation.* The American people will speak by their interests, and they will know who are their friends and who their enemies.

What positions have I held under this government? Beginning with an alderman and running through all branches of the legislature. Some gentleman says I have been a tailor. Now, that did not discomfit me in the least; for when I used to be a tailor I had the reputation of being a good one, and making close fits—always punctual with my customers and always did good work. ... I was saying that I had held nearly all positions, from alderman, through both branches of Congress, to that which I now occupy, and who is there that will say Andrew Johnson ever made a pledge that he did not redeem or made a promise he did not fulfill? Who will say that he has ever acted otherwise than in fidelity to the great mass of the people?

They may talk about beheading and usurpation; but when I am beheaded I want the American people to witness. I do not want by innuendoes, by indirect remarks in high places, to see the man who has assassination brooding in his bosom exclaim, "This presidential obstacle must be gotten out of the way." I make use of a very strong expression when I say that I have no doubt the *intention was to incite assassination* and so get out of the way the obstacle from place and power.

Whether by assassination or not, there are individuals in this government, I doubt not, who want to destroy our institutions and change the character of the government. Are they not satisfied with the blood which has been shed? Does not the murder of Lincoln appease the vengeance and wrath of the opponents of this government? Are they still unslaked? Do they still want more blood? Have they not got honor and courage enough to attain their objects otherwise than by the hands of the assassin? If it is blood they want, let them have courage enough to strike like men. I know they are willing to wound, but they are afraid to strike.

If my blood is to be shed because I vindicate the Union and the preservation of this government in its original purity and character, let it be shed; let an altar to the Union be erected; and then, if it is necessary, take me and lay me upon it, and the blood that now warms and animates my existence shall be poured out as a fit libation to the Union of these states. But let the opponents of this government remember that when it is poured out, "the blood of the martyrs will be the seed of the church."

Gentlemen, this Union will grow—it will continue to increase in strength and power though it may be cemented and cleansed with blood.

DOCUMENT: FOURTEENTH AMENDMENT (1866)

Passed by U.S. Congress June 16, 1866. Ratified July 28, 1868.

Section 1. All persons born or naturalized in the United States and subject to the jurisdiction thereof are citizens of the United States and of the state wherein they reside. No state shall make or enforce any law which shall abridge the privileges or immunities of citizens of the United States; nor shall any state deprive any person of life, liberty, or property without due process of law; nor deny to any person within its jurisdiction the equal protection of the laws.

Section 2. Representatives shall be apportioned among the several states according to their respective numbers, counting the whole number of persons in each state, excluding Indians not taxed. But when the right to vote at any election for the choice of electors for President and Vice-President of the United States, representatives in Congress, the executive and judicial officers of a state, or the members of the legislature thereof, is denied to any of the male inhabitants of such state, being twenty-one years of age, and citizens of the United States, or in any way abridged, except for participation in rebellion or other crime, the basis of representation therein shall be reduced in the proportion which the number of such male citizens shall bear to the whole number of male citizens twenty-one years of age in such state.

Section 3. No person shall be a senator or representative in Congress, or elector of President and Vice-President, or hold any office, civil or military, under the United States, or under any state, who, having previously taken an oath as a member of Congress, or as an officer of the United States, or as a member of any state legislature, or as an executive or judicial officer of any state to support the Constitution of the United States, shall have engaged in insurrection or rebellion against the same or given aid or comfort to the enemies thereof. But Congress may, by a vote of two-thirds of each house, remove such disability.

Section 4. The validity of the public debt of the United States, authorized by law, including debts incurred for payment of pensions and bounties for services in suppressing insurrection or rebellion, shall not be questioned. But neither the United States nor any state shall assume or pay any debt or obligation incurred in aid of insurrection or rebellion against the United States, or any claim for the loss or emancipation of any slave; but all such debts, obligations, and claims shall be held illegal and void.

Section 5. The Congress shall have power to enforce, by appropriate legislation, the provisions of this article.

REPORT OF THE JOINT COMMITTEE ON RECONSTRUCTION (1866)

Source: *Report of the Joint Committee on Reconstruction*, 39 Congress, 1 Session, Washington, 1866, Pt. 3, pp. vii–xxi.

When congress assembled in December last, the people of most of the states lately in rebellion had, under the advice of the President, organized local governments, and some of them had acceded to the terms proposed by him. In his annual message he stated, in general terms, what had been done, but he did not see fit to communicate the details for the information of Congress. While in this and in a subsequent message the President urged the speedy restoration of these states, and expressed the opinion that their condition was such as to justify their restoration, yet it is quite obvious that Congress must either have acted blindly on that opinion of the President, or proceeded to obtain the information requisite for intelligent action on the subject. The impropriety of proceeding wholly on the judgment of any one man, however exalted his station, in a matter involving the welfare of the republic in all future time, or of adopting any plan, coming from any source, without fully understanding all its bearings and comprehending its full effect, was apparent.

The first step, therefore, was to obtain the required information. A call was accordingly made on the President for the information in his possession as to what had been done, in order that Congress might judge for itself as to the grounds of the belief expressed by him in the fitness of states recently in rebellion to participate fully in the conduct of national affairs. This information was not immediately communicated. When the response was finally made, some six weeks after your committee had been in actual session, it was found that the evidence upon which the President seemed to have based his suggestions was incomplete and unsatisfactory. Authenticated

copies of the new constitutions and ordinances adopted by the conventions in three of the states had been submitted, extracts from newspapers furnished scanty information as to the action of one other state, and nothing appears to have been communicated as to the remainder. There was no evidence of the loyalty of those who had participated in these conventions, and in one state alone was any proposition made to submit the action of the conventions to the final judgment of the people. ...

The evidence of an intense hostility to the federal Union, and an equally intense love of the late Confederacy, nurtured by the war, is decisive. While it appears that nearly all are willing to submit, at least for the time being, to the federal authority, it is equally clear that the ruling motive is a desire to obtain the advantages which will be derived from a representation in Congress. Officers of the Union Army, on duty, and Northern men who go South to engage in business, are generally detested and proscribed. Southern men who adhered to the Union are bitterly hated and relentlessly persecuted. In some localities prosecutions have been instituted in state courts against Union officers for acts done in the line of official duty, and similar prosecutions are threatened elsewhere as soon as the United States troops are removed. All such demonstrations show a state of feeling against which it is unmistakably necessary to guard.

The testimony is conclusive that after the collapse of the Confederacy the feeling of the people of the rebellious states was that of abject submission. Having appealed to the tribunal of arms, they had no hope except that, by the magnanimity of their conquerors, their lives, and possibly their property, might be preserved. Unfortunately, the general issue of pardons to persons who had been prominent in the Rebellion, and the feeling of kindliness and conciliation manifested by the executive, and very generally indicated through the Northern press, had the effect to render whole communities forgetful of the crime they had committed, defiant toward the federal government, and regardless of their duties as citizens.

The conciliatory measures of the government do not seem to have been met even halfway. The bitterness and defiance exhibited toward the United States under such circumstances is without a parallel in the history of the world. In return for our leniency we receive only an insulting denial of our authority. In return for our kind desire for the resumption of fraternal relations we receive only an insolent assumption of rights and privileges long since forfeited. The crime we have punished is paraded as a virtue, and the principles of republican government which we have vindicated at so terrible a cost are denounced as unjust and oppressive.

If we add to this evidence the fact that, although peace has been declared by the President, he has not, to this day, deemed it safe to restore the writ of habeas corpus, to relieve the insurrectionary states

of martial law, nor to withdraw the troops from many localities, and that the commanding general deems an increase of the army indispensable to the preservation of order and the protection of loyal and well-disposed people in the South, the proof of a condition of feeling hostile to the Union and dangerous to the government throughout the insurrectionary states would seem to be overwhelming.

With such evidence before them, it is the opinion of your committee:

- That the states lately in rebellion were, at the close of the war, disorganized communities, without civil government, and without constitutions or other forms, by virtue of which political relations could legally exist between them and the federal government.
- That Congress cannot be expected to recognize as valid the election of representatives from disorganized communities, which, from the very nature of the case, were unable to present their claim to representation under those established and recognized rules, the observance of which has been hitherto required.
- That Congress would not be justified in admitting such communities to a participation in the government of the country without first providing such constitutional or other guarantees as will tend to secure the civil rights of all citizens of the

republic; a just equality of representation; protection against claims founded in rebellion and crime; a temporary restoration of the right of suffrage to those who have not actively participated in the efforts to destroy the Union and overthrow the government, and the exclusion from positions of public trust of, at least, a portion of those whose crimes have proved them to be enemies to the Union and unworthy of public confidence.

Your committee will, perhaps, hardly be deemed excusable for extending this report further; but inasmuch as immediate and unconditional representation of the states lately in rebellion is demanded as a matter of right, and delay and even hesitation is denounced as grossly oppressive and unjust, as well as unwise and impolitic, it may not be amiss again to call attention to a few undisputed and notorious facts, and the principles of public law applicable thereto, in order that the propriety of that claim may be fully considered and well understood.

The state of Tennessee occupies a position distinct from all the other insurrectionary states, and has been the subject of a separate report, which your committee have not thought it expedient to disturb. Whether Congress shall see fit to make that state the subject of separate action, or to include it in the same category with all others so far as concerns the imposition of preliminary conditions,

it is not within the province of this committee either to determine or advise.

To ascertain whether any of the so-called Confederate States "are entitled to be represented in either house of Congress," the essential inquiry is, whether there is, in any one of them, a constituency qualified to be represented in Congress. The question how far persons claiming seats in either house possess the credentials necessary to enable them to represent a duly qualified constituency is one for the consideration of each house separately, after the preliminary question shall have been finally determined.

We now propose to restate, as briefly as possible, the general facts and principles applicable to all the states recently in rebellion:

First. The seats of the senators and representatives from the so-called Confederate States became vacant in the year 1861, during the second session of the Thirty-sixth Congress, by the voluntary withdrawal of their incumbents, with the sanction and by direction of the legislatures or conventions of their respective states. This was done as a hostile act against the Constitution and government of the United States, with a declared intent to overthrow the same by forming a Southern confederation. This act of declared hostility was speedily followed by an organization of the same states into a Confederacy, which levied and waged war, by sea and land, against the United States.

This war continued more than four years, within which period the Rebel armies besieged the national capital, invaded the loyal states, burned their towns and cities, robbed their citizens, destroyed more than 250,000 loyal soldiers, and imposed an increased national burden of not less than $3,500 million, of which $700 million or $800 million have already been met and paid. From the time these confederated states thus withdrew their representation in Congress and levied war against the United States, the great mass of their people became and were insurgents, rebels, traitors, and all of them assumed and occupied the political, legal, and practical relation of enemies of the United States. This position is established by acts of Congress and judicial decisions, and is recognized repeatedly by the President in public proclamations, documents, and speeches.

Second. The states thus confederated prosecuted their war against the United States to final arbitrament, and did not cease until all their armies were captured, their military power destroyed, their civil officers, state and confederate, taken prisoners or put to flight, every vestige of state and confederate government obliterated, their territory overrun and occupied by the federal armies, and their people reduced to the condition of enemies conquered in war, entitled only by public law to such rights, privileges, and conditions as might be vouchsafed by the conqueror. This position is also established by judicial decisions, and is recognized by the President in public proclamations, documents, and speeches.

Third. Having voluntarily deprived themselves of representation in Congress for the criminal purpose of destroying the Federal Union, and having reduced themselves, by the act of levying war, to the condition of public enemies, they have no right to complain of temporary exclusion from Congress; but, on the contrary, having voluntarily renounced the right to representation, and disqualified themselves by crime from participating in the government, the burden now rests upon them, before claiming to be reinstated in their former condition, to show that they are qualified to resume federal relations. In order to do this, they must prove that they have established, with the consent of the people, republican forms of government in harmony with the Constitution and laws of the United States, that all hostile purposes have ceased, and should give adequate guarantees against future treason and rebellion—guarantees which shall prove satisfactory to the government against which they rebelled, and by whose arms they were subdued.

Fourth. Having, by this treasonable withdrawal from Congress, and by flagrant rebellion and war, forfeited all civil and political rights and privileges under the Federal Constitution, they can only be restored thereto by the permission and authority of that constitutional power against which they rebelled and by which they were subdued.

Fifth. These rebellious enemies were conquered by the people of the United States, acting through all the coordinate branches of the government, and not by the Executive Department alone. The powers of conqueror are not so vested in the President that he can fix and regulate the terms of settlement and confer congressional representation on conquered rebels and traitors. Nor can he, in any way, qualify enemies of the government to exercise its lawmaking power. The authority to restore rebels to political power in the federal government can be exercised only with the concurrence of all the departments in which political power is vested; and hence the several proclamations of the President to the people of the Confederate States cannot be considered as extending beyond the purposes declared, and can only be regarded as provisional permission by the commander in chief of the army to do certain acts, the effect and validity whereof is to be determined by the constitutional government, and not solely by the executive power.

Sixth. The question before Congress is, then, whether conquered enemies have the right, and shall be permitted at their own pleasure and on their own terms, to participate in making laws for their conquerors; whether conquered Rebels may change their theater of operations from the battlefield, where they were defeated and overthrown, to the halls of Congress, and, through their representatives, seize upon the government which they fought to destroy; whether the national Treasury, the Army of the nation, its Navy, its forts and arsenals, its whole civil administration, its credit, its pensioners, the widows and orphans of those who perished in the war, the public honor, peace and safety, shall all be turned over to the keeping of its recent enemies without delay, and without imposing such conditions as, in the opinion of Congress, the security of the country and its institutions may demand.

Seventh. The history of mankind exhibits no example of such madness and folly. The instinct of self-preservation protests against it. The surrender by Grant to Lee, and by Sherman to Johnston, would have been disasters of less magnitude, for new armies could have been raised, new battles fought, and the government saved. The anticoercive policy, which, under pretext of avoiding bloodshed, allowed the rebellion to take form and gather force, would be surpassed in infamy by the matchless wickedness that would now surrender the halls of Congress to those so recently in rebellion until proper precautions shall have been taken to secure the national faith and the national safety.

Eighth. As has been shown in this report, and in the evidence submitted, no proof has been afforded to Congress of a constituency in any one of the so-called Confederate States, unless we except the state of Tennessee, qualified to elect senators and representatives in Congress. No state constitution, or amendment to a state constitution, has had the sanction of the people. All the so-called legislation of state conventions and legislatures has been had under military dictation. If the President may, at his will, and under his own authority, whether as military commander or chief executive, qualify persons to appoint senators and elect representatives, and empower others to appoint and elect them, he thereby practically controls the organization of the Legislative Department. The constitutional form of government is thereby practically destroyed, and its powers absorbed in the executive. And while your committee do not for a moment impute to the President any such design, but cheerfully concede to him the most patriotic motives, they cannot but look with alarm upon a precedent so fraught with danger to the republic.

Ninth. The necessity of providing adequate safeguards for the future, before restoring the insurrectionary states to a participation in the direction of public affairs, is apparent from the bitter hostility to the government and people of the United States yet existing throughout the conquered territory, as proved incontestably by the testimony of many witnesses and by undisputed facts.

Tenth. The conclusion of your committee, therefore, is that the so-called Confederate States are not, at present, entitled to representation in the Congress of the United States; that, before allowing such representation, adequate security for future peace and safety should be required; that this can only be found in such changes of the organic law as shall determine the civil rights and privileges of all citizens in all parts of the republic, shall place representation on an equitable basis, shall fix a stigma upon treason, and protect the loyal people against future claims for the expenses incurred in support of rebellion and for manumitted slaves, together with an express grant of power in Congress to enforce those provisions. To this end they offer a joint resolution for amending the Constitution of the United States, and the two several bills designed to carry the same into effect, before referred to.

Before closing this report, your committee beg leave to state that the specific recommendations submitted by them are the result of mutual concession, after a long and careful comparison of conflicting opinions. Upon a question of such magnitude, infinitely important as it is to the future of the republic, it was not to be expected that all should think alike. Sensible of the imperfections of the scheme, your committee submit it to Congress as the best they could agree upon, in the hope that its imperfections may be cured, and its deficiencies supplied, by legislative wisdom; and that, when finally adopted, it may tend to restore peace and harmony to the whole country, and to place our republican institutions on a more stable foundation.

FEDERAL GRAND JURY REPORT ON THE KU KLUX KLAN (1871)

Source: 42 Congress, 2 Session, House Report No. 22, Pt. 1, pp. 48–49.

In closing the labors of the present term, the grand jury beg leave to submit the following presentment.

During the whole session we have been engaged in investigations of the most grave and extraordinary character—investigations of the crimes committed by the organization known as the Ku Klux Klan. The evidence elicited has been voluminous, gathered from the victims themselves and their families, as well as those who belong to the Klan and participated in its crimes. The jury has been shocked beyond measure at the developments which have been made in their presence of the number and character of the atrocities committed, producing a state of terror and a sense of utter insecurity among a large portion of the people, especially the colored population. The evidence produced before us has established the following facts:

- That there has existed since 1868, in many counties of the state, an organization known as the "Ku Klux Klan," or "Invisible Empire of the South," which embraces in its membership a large proportion of the white population of every profession and class.
- That this Klan [is] bound together by an oath, administered to its members at the time of their initiation into the order, of which the following is a copy:

OBLIGATION

I [name], before the immaculate Judge of Heaven and earth, and upon the Holy Evangelists of Almighty God,

do, of my own free will and accord, subscribe to the following sacredly binding obligation:

- We are on the side of justice, humanity, and constitutional liberty, as bequeathed to us in its purity by our forefathers.
- We oppose and reject the principles of the Radical Party.
- We pledge mutual aid to each other in sickness, distress, and pecuniary embarrassment.
- Female friends, widows, and their households shall ever be special objects of our regard and protection.

Any member divulging, or causing to be divulged, any of the foregoing obligations, shall meet the fearful penalty and traitor's doom, which is Death! Death! Death!

- That, in addition to this oath, the Klan has a constitution and bylaws, which provides, among other things, that each member shall furnish himself with a pistol, a Ku Klux gown, and a signal instrument.
- That the operations of the Klan were executed in the night, and were invariably directed against members of the Republican Party by warnings to leave the country, by whippings, and by murder.
- That in large portions of the counties of York, Union, and

Spartanburgh, to which our attention has been more particularly called in our investigations during part of the time for the last eighteen months, the civil law has been set at defiance and ceased to afford any protection to the citizens.

- That the Klan, in carrying out the purposes for which it was organized and armed, inflicted summary vengeance on the colored citizens of these counties by breaking into their houses at the dead of night, dragging them from their beds, torturing them in the most inhuman manner, and in many instances murdering them; and this, mainly, on account of their political affiliations. Occasionally, additional reasons operated, but in no instance was the political feature wanting.

- That for this condition of things, for all these violations of law and order and the sacred rights of citizens, many of the leading men of those counties were responsible. It was proven that large numbers of the most prominent citizens were members of the order. Many of this class attended meetings of the Grand Klan. At a meeting of the Grand Klan held in Spartanburgh County, at which there were representatives from the various dens of Spartanburgh, York, Union, and Chester counties, in this state, besides a

number from North Carolina, a resolution was adopted that no raids should be undertaken or anyone whipped or injured by members of the Klan without orders from the Grand Klan. The penalty for violating this resolution was 100 lashes on the bare back for the first offense; and for the second, death.

This testimony establishes the nature of the discipline enforced in the order, and also the fact that many of the men who were openly and publicly speaking against the Klan, and pretending to deplore the work of this murderous conspiracy, were influential members of the order and directing its operations, even in detail.

The jury has been appalled as much at the number of outrages as at their character, it appearing that 11 murders and over 600 whippings have been committed in York County alone. Our investigation in regard to the other counties named has been less full; but it is believed, from the testimony, that an equal or greater number has been committed in Union, and that the number is not greatly less in Spartanburgh and Laurens.

We are of the opinion that the most vigorous prosecution of the parties implicated in these crimes is imperatively demanded; that without this there is great danger that these outrages will be continued, and that there will be no security to our fellow citizens of African descent.

We would say further that unless the strong arm of the government is interposed to punish these crimes committed upon this class of citizens, there is every reason to believe that an organized and determined attempt at retaliation will be made, which can only result in a state of anarchy and bloodshed too horrible to contemplate.

FREDERICK DOUGLASS: THE COLOUR LINE IN AMERICA (1883)

Source: *Three Addresses on the Relations Subsisting Between the White and Colored People of the United States*, Washington, 1886, pp. 3–23.

It is our lot to live among a people whose laws, traditions, and prejudices have been against us for centuries, and from these they are not yet free. To assume that they are free from these evils simply because they have changed their laws is to assume what is utterly unreasonable and contrary to facts. Large bodies move slowly. Individuals may be converted on the instant and change their whole course of life. Nations never. Time and events are required for the conversion of nations. Not even the character of a great political organization can be changed by a new platform. It will be the same old snake though in a new skin.

Though we have had war, reconstruction, and abolition as a nation, we still linger in the shadow and blight of an extinct institution. Though the colored man is no longer subject to be bought and sold, he is still surrounded by an adverse sentiment which fetters all his movements. In his downward course he meets with no resistance, but his course upward is resented and resisted at every step of his progress. If he comes in ignorance, rags, and wretchedness, he conforms to the popular belief of his character, and in that character he is welcome. But if he shall come as a gentleman, a scholar, and a statesman, he is hailed as a contradiction to the national faith concerning his race, and his coming is resented as impudence. In the one case he may provoke contempt and derision, but in the other he is an affront to pride and provokes malice. Let him do what he will, there is at present, therefore, no escape for him. The color line meets him everywhere, and in a measure shuts him out from all respectable and profitable trades and callings.

In spite of all your religion and laws, he is a rejected man. He is rejected by trade unions of every trade, and refused work while he lives and burial when he dies; and yet he is asked to forget his color and forget that which everybody else remembers. If he offers himself to a builder as a mechanic, to a client as a lawyer, to a patient as a physician, to a college as a professor, to a firm as a clerk, to a government department as an agent or an officer, he is sternly met on the color line, and his claim to consideration in some way is disputed on the ground of color.

Not even our churches, whose members profess to follow the despised Nazarene, whose home, when on earth, was among the lowly and despised, have yet conquered this feeling of color madness, and what is true of our churches is also true of our courts of law. Neither is free from this all-pervading atmosphere of color hate. The one describes the Deity as impartial, no respecter of persons, and the other the Goddess of Justice as blindfolded, with sword by her side and scales in her hand, held evenly between high and low, rich and poor, white and black; but both are the images of American imagination rather than American practices.

Taking advantage of the general disposition in this country to impute crime to color, white men *color* their faces to commit crime and wash off the hated color to escape punishment. In many places where the commission of crime is alleged against one of our color, the ordinary processes of the law are set aside as too slow for the impetuous justice of the infuriated populace. They take the law into their own bloody hands and proceed to whip, stab, shoot, hang, or burn the alleged culprit, without the intervention of courts, counsel, judges, juries, or witnesses. In such cases it is not the business of the accusers to prove guilt, but it is for the accused to prove his innocence, a thing hard for any man to do, even in a court of law, and utterly impossible for him to do in these infernal lynch courts.

A man accused, surprised, frightened, and captured by a motley crowd, dragged with a rope around his neck in midnight-darkness to the nearest tree, and told in the coarsest terms of profanity to prepare for death, would be more than human if he did not, in his terror-stricken appearance, more confirm suspicion of guilt than the contrary. Worse still, in the presence of such hell-black outrages, the pulpit is usually dumb, and the press in the neighborhood is silent or openly takes sides with the mob. There are occasional cases in which white men are lynched, but one sparrow does not make a summer. Everyone knows that what is called lynch law is peculiarly the law for colored people and for nobody else.

If there were no other grievance than this horrible and barbarous lynch-law custom, we should be justified in assembling, as we have now done, to expose and denounce it. But this is not all. Even now, after twenty years of so-called emancipation, we are subject to lawless raids of midnight riders, who, with blackened faces, invade our homes and perpetrate the foulest of crimes upon us and our families. This condition of things is too flagrant and notorious to require specifications or proof. Thus in all the relations of life and death we are met by the color line. We cannot ignore it if we would, and ought not if we could. It hunts us at midnight, it denies us accommodation in hotels and justice in the courts; excludes our children from schools, refuses our sons the chance to learn trades, and compels us to pursue only such labor as will bring the least reward.

While we recognize the color line as a hurtful force, a mountain barrier to our progress, wounding our bleeding feet with its flinty rocks at every step, we do not despair. We are a hopeful people.

This convention is a proof of our faith in you, in reason, in truth, and justice; our belief that prejudice, with all its malign accompaniments, may yet be removed by peaceful means; that, assisted by time and events and the growing enlightenment of both races, the color line will ultimately become harmless. When this shall come it will then only be used, as it should be, to distinguish one variety of the human family from another. It will cease to have any civil, political, or moral significance, and colored conventions will then be dispensed with as anachronisms, wholly out of place—but not till then.

Do not marvel that we are not discouraged. The faith within us has a rational basis and is confirmed by facts. When we consider how deep-seated this feeling against us is; the long centuries it has been forming; the forces of avarice which have been marshaled to sustain it; how the language and literature of the country have been pervaded with it; how the church, the press, the playhouse, and other influences of the country have been arrayed in its support, the progress toward its extinction must be considered vast and wonderful.

If liberty, with us, is yet but a name, our citizenship is but a sham, and our suffrage thus far only a cruel mockery, we may yet congratulate ourselves upon the fact that the laws and institutions of the country are sound, just, and liberal. There is hope for a people when their laws are righteous, whether for the moment they conform to their requirements or not. But until this nation shall make its practice accord with its Constitution and its righteous laws, it will not do to reproach the colored people of this country with keeping up the color line; for that people would prove themselves scarcely worthy of even theoretical freedom, to say nothing of practical freedom, if they settled down in silent, servile, and cowardly submission to their wrongs from fear of making their color visible.

They are bound by every element of manhood to hold conventions in their own name and on their own behalf, to keep their grievances before the people and make every organized protest against the wrongs inflicted upon them within their power. They should scorn the counsels of cowards and hang their banner on the outer wall. Who would be free, themselves must strike the blow. We do not believe, as we are often told, that the Negro is the ugly child of the national family, and the more he is kept out of sight the better it will be for him. You know that liberty given is never so precious as liberty sought for and fought for. The man outraged is the man to make the outcry. Depend upon it, men will not care much for a people who do not care for themselves.

Our meeting here was opposed by some of our members because it would disturb the peace of the Republican Party. The suggestion came from coward lips and misapprehended the character of that party. If the Republican Party cannot stand a demand for justice and fair play, it ought to go down. We were men before that party was born, and our manhood is more sacred than any party can be. Parties were made for men, not men for parties.

If the 6 million colored people of this country, armed with the Constitution of the United States, with a million votes of their own to lean upon and millions of white men at their back, whose hearts are responsive to the claims of humanity, have not sufficient spirit and wisdom to organize and combine to defend themselves from outrage, discrimination, and oppression, it will be idle for them to expect that the Republican Party or any other political party will organize and combine for them or care what becomes of them. Men may combine to prevent cruelty to animals, for they are dumb and cannot speak for themselves; but we are men and must speak for ourselves, or we shall not be spoken for at all. We have conventions in America for Ireland, but we should have none if Ireland did not speak for herself. It is because she makes a noise and keeps her cause before the people that other people go to her help. It was the sword of Washington and of Lafayette that gave us independence.

In conclusion upon this color objection, we have to say that we meet here in open daylight. There is nothing sinister about us. The eyes of the nation are upon us. Ten thousand newspapers may tell if they choose of whatever is said and done here. They may commend our wisdom or condemn our folly, precisely as we shall be wise or foolish. We put ourselves before them as honest men and ask their judgment upon our work.

BOOKER T. WASHINGTON: THE ROAD TO AFRICAN AMERICAN PROGRESS (1895)

Source: *The Story of My Life and Work*, Revised edition, Naperville, Ill., and Atlanta, Ga., 1900, pp. 165–171.

Mr. President and Gentlemen of the Board of Directors and Citizens:

One-third of the population of the South is of the Negro race. No enterprise seeking the material, civil, or moral welfare of this section can disregard this element of our population and reach the highest success. I but convey to you, Mr. President and Directors, the sentiment of the masses of my race when I say that in no way have the value and manhood of the American Negro been more fittingly and generously recognized than by the managers of this magnificent exposition at every stage of its progress. It is a recognition that will do more to cement the friendship of the two races than any occurrence since the dawn of our freedom.

Not only this, but the opportunity here afforded will awaken among us a new era of industrial progress. Ignorant and inexperienced, it is not strange that in the first years of our new life we began at the top instead of at the bottom; that a seat in Congress or the state legislature was more sought than real estate or industrial skill; that the political convention or stump speaking had more attractions than starting a dairy farm or truck garden.

A ship lost at sea for many days suddenly sighted a friendly vessel. From the mast of the unfortunate vessel was seen a signal: "Water, water; we die of thirst." The answer from the friendly vessel at once came back: "Cast down your bucket where you are." A second time the signal, "Water, water, send us water!" ran up from the distressed vessel, and was answered: "Cast down your bucket where you are." And a third and fourth signal for water was answered: "Cast down your bucket where you are." The captain of the distressed vessel, at last heeding the injunction, cast down his bucket, and it came up full of fresh, sparkling water from the mouth of the Amazon River.

To those of my race who depend on bettering their condition in a foreign land or who underestimate the importance of cultivating friendly relations with the Southern white man, who is their next-door neighbor, I would say: Cast down your bucket where you are; cast it down in making friends, in every manly way, of the people of all races by whom we are surrounded. Cast it down in agriculture, mechanics, in commerce, in domestic service, and in the professions. And in this connection it is well to bear in mind that whatever other sins the South may be called to bear, when it comes to business, pure and simple, it is in the South that the Negro is given a man's chance in the commercial world, and in nothing is this exposition more eloquent than in emphasizing this chance.

Our greatest danger is that, in the great leap from slavery to freedom, we may overlook the fact that the masses of us are to live by the productions of our hands and fail to keep in mind that we shall prosper in proportion as we learn to dignify and glorify common labor, and put brains and skill into the common occupations of life; shall prosper in proportion as we learn to draw the line between the superficial and the substantial, the ornamental gewgaws of life and the useful. No race can prosper till it learns that there is as much dignity in tilling a field as in writing a poem. It is at the bottom of life we must begin, and not at the top. Nor should we permit our grievances to overshadow our opportunities.

To those of the white race who look to the incoming of those of foreign birth and strange tongue and habits for the prosperity of the South, were I permitted I would repeat what I say to my own race, "Cast down your bucket where you are." Cast it down among the 8 million Negroes whose habits you know, whose fidelity and love you have tested in days when to have proved treacherous meant the ruin of your firesides. Cast down your bucket among these people who have, without strikes and labor wars, tilled your fields, cleared your forests, builded your railroads and cities, and brought forth treasures from the bowels of the earth and helped make possible this magnificent representation of the progress of the South. Casting down your bucket among my people, helping and encouraging them as you are doing on these grounds, and, with education of head, hand, and heart, you will find that they will buy your surplus land, make blossom the waste places in your fields, and run your factories.

While doing this, you can be sure in the future, as in the past, that you and your families will be surrounded by the most patient, faithful, law-abiding, and unresentful people that the world has seen. As we have proved our loyalty to you in the past, in nursing your children, watching by the sickbed of your mothers and fathers, and often following them with tear-dimmed eyes to their graves, so in the future, in our humble way, we shall stand by you with a devotion that no foreigner can approach, ready to lay down our lives, if need be, in defense of yours; interlacing our industrial, commercial, civil, and religious life with yours in a way that shall make the interests of both races one. In all things that are purely social we can be as separate as the fingers, yet one as the hand in all things essential to mutual progress.

There is no defense or security for any of us except in the highest intelligence and development of all. If anywhere there are efforts tending to curtail the fullest growth of the Negro, let these efforts be turned into stimulating, encouraging, and making him the most useful and intelligent citizen. Effort or means so invested will pay a thousand percent interest. These efforts will be twice blessed—"blessing him that gives and him that takes."

There is no escape, through law of man or God, from the inevitable:

The laws of changeless justice bind
Oppressor with oppressed;
And close as sin and suffering joined
We march to fate abreast.

Nearly 16 million hands will aid you in pulling the load upward, or they will pull against you the load downward. We shall constitute one-third and more of the ignorance and crime of the South, or one-third its intelligence and progress; we shall contribute one-third to the business and industrial prosperity of the South, or we shall prove a veritable body of death, stagnating, depressing, retarding every effort to advance the body politic.

Gentlemen of the exposition, as we present to you our humble effort at an exhibition of our progress, you must not expect overmuch. Starting thirty years ago with ownership here and there in a few quilts and pumpkins and chickens (gathered from miscellaneous sources), remember: the path that has led from these to the invention and production of agricultural implements, buggies, steam engines, newspapers, books, statuary, carving, paintings, the management of drugstores and banks, has not been trodden without contact with thorns and thistles. While we take pride in what we exhibit as a result of our independent efforts, we do not for a moment forget that our part in this exhibition would fall far short of your expectations but for the constant help that has come to our educational life, not only from the Southern states but especially from Northern philanthropists who have made their gifts a constant stream of blessing and encouragement.

The wisest among my race understand that the agitation of questions of social equality is the extremest folly, and that progress in the enjoyment of all the privileges that will come to us must be the result of severe and constant struggle rather than of artificial forcing. No race that has anything to contribute to the markets of the world is long in any degree ostracized. It is important and right that all privileges of the law be ours, but it is vastly more important that we be prepared for the exercise of those privileges. The opportunity to earn a dollar in a factory just now is worth infinitely more than the opportunity to spend a dollar in an opera house.

In conclusion, may I repeat that nothing in thirty years has given us more hope and encouragement and drawn us so near to you of the white race as this opportunity offered by the exposition; and here bending, as it were, over the altar that represents the results of the struggles of your race and mine, both starting practically empty-handed three decades ago, I pledge that, in your effort to work out the great and intricate problem which God has laid at the doors of the South, you shall have at all times the patient, sympathetic help of my race; only let this be constantly in mind that, while from representations in these buildings of the product of field, of forest, of mine, of factory, letters, and art, much good will come—yet far above and beyond material benefits will be that higher good, that let us pray God will come, in a blotting out of sectional differences and racial animosities and suspicions, in a determination to administer absolute justice, in a willing obedience among all classes to the mandates of law. This, coupled with our material prosperity, will bring into our beloved South a new heaven and a new earth.

GLOSSARY

abjure To reject solemnly.

aforesaid Mentioned previously.

approbation An act of approving formally or officially.

arraign To accuse of wrong, inadequacy, or imperfection.

artisan A worker who practices a trade or handicraft.

attaché A technical expert on a country's diplomatic staff at a foreign capital.

aught Anything.

cabal A small number of persons organized for the purpose of engaging in secret or private intrigue, as in a plot to overturn a government.

calumniate To injure the reputation of by uttering false charges or misrepresentations; to slander.

Cerberian Of or related to Cerberus, a 3-headed dog that in Greek mythology guards the entrance to Hades.

commutation fee The fee a draftee pays in lieu of military service.

conciliate To become friendly or agreeable.

consecrate To make or declare sacred.

consummate adj. Of the highest degree.

consummate v. Finish, complete.

countervailing Counteracting.

defalcation The act or an instance of embezzling.

defile To march off in a line.

delineate To describe, portray, or set forth with accuracy or in detail.

demur Delay; hesitate.

deprecate To express disapproval of.

deringer Also spelled derringer, a short-barrelled pocket pistol produced in the early 19th century by Philadelphia gunsmith Henry Deringer.

dissipate To cause to spread thin or scatter and gradually vanish.

doctrine A principle of law established through past decisions.

ethnogenesis The process of developing an ethnic identity.

ex post facto Done, made, or formulated after the fact.

extol To praise highly.

fain With pleasure; gladly.

fait accompli A thing accomplished and presumably irreversible.

fetter Something that confines or restrains, as a chain or shackle for the feet.

grandfather clause A formal stipulation creating an exemption based on circumstances previously existing; especially a provision in several Southern state constitutions designed to enfranchise poor whites and disenfranchise blacks by waiving high voting requirements for descendants of men voting before 1867.

habeas corpus Any of several common-law writs issued to bring a party before a court or judge.

hegemony Preponderant influence or authority over others.

impromptu Made, done, or formed on or as if on the spur of the moment.

incendiary A person who excites factions, quarrels, or sedition.

indemnify To secure against hurt, loss, or damage.

insurrection An act or instance of revolting against civil authority or an established government.

inveigh To protest or complain bitterly or vehemently.

ironclad An armoured naval vessel especially of the mid- to late 19th century.

laudable Worthy of praise; commendable.

manifesto A written statement declaring publicly the intentions, motives, or views of its issuer.

manumit To release from slavery.

obdurate Resistant to persuasion or softening influences.

pap Originally meaning a soft food for infants, the term came to represent a simple discourse felt to be suitable only for the minds of infants.

parish A civil division of the state of Louisiana corresponding to a county in other states.

partisan A firm adherent to a party, faction, cause, or person.

Pharisaic Strictly speaking, the term refers to the Pharisees, an ancient Jewish sect noted for rigid observance of rites and ceremonies of the written law and for insistence on the validity of their own oral traditions concerning the law. In common parlance, the term refers to one who makes an outward show of piety and morality but lacks inward spirit.

pocket veto A tactic used by presidents to quash a bill seen as objectionable. If said bill is sent within days of an adjournment of Congress, the president simply "pockets"—and therefore nullifies—the bill by failing to return it to Congress before the session ends.

poniard A dagger with a usually slender blade of triangular or square cross section.

portentous Ominous or foreshadowing.

posterity All future generations.

provincialism The quality or state of having local or restricted interests or outlooks.

quixotic Foolishly impractical, especially in the pursuit of ideals.

reconnaissance A preliminary survey to gain information, especially an exploratory military survey of enemy territory.

rhetorician An eloquent or linguistically lofty writer or speaker.

roseate Overly optimistic; viewed favourably.

scalawag A pejorative term for a white Southerner acting in support of the Reconstruction governments after the American Civil War.

schism Division; separation.

sharecropper A tenant farmer, especially in the American South, who is provided with credit for seed, tools, living quarters, and food. Sharecroppers work the land, receiving an agreed share of the value of the crop minus charges.

shibboleth A custom or usage regarded as distinguishing one group from others.

stratum A socioeconomic level of society comprising persons of the same or similar status especially with regard to education or culture.

succor Aid; help.

suffrage The right of voting.

tenderfooted Timid.

thenceforward Onward from that place or time.

thither To that place; there.

trellis To cross or interlace on or through; interweave.

usurp To seize and hold (as office, place, or powers) in possession by force or without right.

usury Interest in excess of a legal rate charged to a borrower for the use of money.

visage The face, countenance, or appearance of a person or sometimes an animal.

vouchsafe To grant as a privilege or special favour.

whither To what place.

writ A formal legal document.

THE CIVIL WAR

James M. McPherson, *Battle Cry of Freedom* (1988), is an engrossing narrative history of the Civil War. John Keegan, *The American Civil War: A Military History* (2010), is an examination of the war by an eminent military historian. James M. McPherson, *Tried by War: Abraham Lincoln as Commander in Chief* (2008), assesses Lincoln's role in the military conduct of the war; Doris Kearns Goodwin, *Team of Rivals: The Political Genius of Abraham Lincoln* (2005), is an engrossing account of Lincoln's skillful exploitation of a cabinet made up of political heavyweights who initially questioned his ability to lead. Jennifer Weber, *Copperheads: The Rise and Fall of Lincoln's Opponents in the North* (2006), explores the political challenges Lincoln faced on the home front during the war. Drew Gilpin Faust, *This Republic of Suffering: Death and the American Civil War* (2008), studies the consequences of total war on the United States and the national psyche.

Other syntheses of modern scholarship are James M. McPherson, *Ordeal by Fire* (1982); and J.G. Randall and David Donald, *The Civil War and Reconstruction*, 2nd ed. rev. (1969). Allan Nevins, *Ordeal of the Union*, 8 vol. (1947–71), provides a comprehensive history. Clement Eaton, *A History of the Old South*, 3rd ed. (1975, reissued 1988), is a general history of the region. A perceptive account of the political conflicts of the late 1850s is Roy F. Nichols, *The Disruption of American Democracy* (1948, reissued 1967); while Don E. Fehrenbacher, *The Dred Scott Case* (1978), offers an analysis of the constitutional issues. Jean H. Baker, *Affairs of Party* (1983), discusses the strong partisan attachments of ordinary citizens. Comprehensive coverage of the Confederate military effort in the East is Douglas Southall Freeman, *Lee's Lieutenants, a Study in Command*, 3 vol. (1942–44, reissued 1970–72); while Warren W. Hassler, Jr., *Commanders of the Army of the Potomac* (1962, reprinted 1979), does the same for the Federals. Charles Bracelen Flood, *Grant and Sherman: The Friendship That Won the Civil War* (2005), looks at one of the war's most pivotal military partnerships. Joseph Harsh, *Taken at the Flood: Robert E. Lee and Confederate Strategy in the Maryland Campaign of 1862* (1999), provides insight into this important chapter of the war. Studies of the war in the Mississippi Valley include Thomas L. Connelly, *Army of the Heartland: The Army of Tennessee, 1861–1862* (1967), and *Autumn of Glory: The Army of Tennessee, 1862–1865* (1971). An examination of the Gettysburg battle is Edwin B. Coddington, *The Gettysburg Campaign: A Study in Command* (1968, reissued 1984). Winston Groom, *Vicksburg, 1863* (2009), details the events around the siege of Vicksburg. Virgil

Carrington Jones, *The Civil War at Sea*, 3 vol. (1960–62), describes the naval war.

RECONSTRUCTION

The most comprehensive modern account of Reconstruction is Eric Foner, *Reconstruction: America's Unfinished Revolution, 1863–1877* (1988), also available in an abridged version, *A Short History of Reconstruction* (1990). Leon F. Litwack explores African American aspirations immediately following emancipation in *Been in the Storm So Long: The Aftermath of Slavery* (1979). Steven Hahn, *A Nation Under Our Feet: Black Political Struggles in the Rural South from Slavery to the Great Migration* (2003), discusses grassroots black politics. Eric Foner, *Freedom's Lawmakers: A Directory of Black Officeholders During Reconstruction* (rev. ed., 1996), offers biographical sketches of more than 1,500 black officials. George C. Rable, *But There Was No Peace: The Role of Violence in the Politics of Reconstruction* (1984), examines the Ku Klux Klan and other terrorist organizations. Heather Cox Richardson, *The Death of Reconstruction: Race, Labor, and Politics in the Post-Civil War North, 1865–1901* (2001), discusses the retreat from Reconstruction. Still worth reading is W.E.B. Du Bois, *Black Reconstruction in America* (1935), a pioneering critique of the old racist view of the period.

Excellent syntheses of scholarship on the Reconstruction period are Rembert W. Patrick, *The Reconstruction of the Nation* (1967); John Hope Franklin, *Reconstruction* (1961); and Kenneth M. Stampp, *The Era of Reconstruction, 1865–1877* (1965, reprinted 1975). C. Vann Woodward, *Reunion and Reaction* (1951, reissued 1966), covers behind-the-scenes political and economic negotiations in the disputed 1876–77 election. A definitive account of the South in the post-Reconstruction era is C. Vann Woodward, *Origins of the New South, 1877–1913* (1951, reissued 1971). Important studies of postwar race relations include C. Vann Woodward, *The Strange Career of Jim Crow*, 3rd rev. ed. (1974, reissued 1982); and Joel Williamson, *The Crucible of Race* (1984).

INDEX